ADVENTURES

with the

WORD OF GOD

REBECCA IRVIN

ADVENTURES

with the

WORD OF GOD

MAKING SCRIPTURE STUDY EXCITING
FOR THE ENTIRE FAMILY

Horizon Publishers
Springville, Utah

This is not an official publication of The Church of Jesus Christ of Latter-day Saints. The opinions and views expressed herein belong solely to the author and do not necessarily represent the opinions or views of Cedar Fort, Inc. Permission for the use of sources, graphics, and photos is also solely the responsibility of the author.

ISBN 13: 978-0-88290-845-8

Published by Horizon Publishers, an imprint of Cedar Fort, Inc., 2373 W. 700 S., Springville, UT 84663
Distributed by Cedar Fort, Inc., www.cedarfort.com

LIBRARY OF CONGRESS CATALOGING-IN-PUBLICATION DATA

Irvine, Rebecca, 1970–
  Adventures with the Word of God : making scripture study exciting for the
entire family / Rebecca Irvine.
    p. cm.
  ISBN 978-0-88290-845-8
  1. Church of Jesus Christ of Latter day Saints—Doctrines—Study and
teaching. 2. Mormon Church—Doctrines—Study and teaching. 3.
Bible—Study and teaching. 4. Family—Religious life. 5. Religious
education—Activity programs. 6. Christian education—Home training. I.
Title.
  BX8610.I78 2008
  249—dc22
                              2008005235

Cover design by Angela Olsen
Cover design © 2008 by Lyle Mortimer
Edited and typeset by Annaliese B. Cox

Printed in the United States of America

10 9 8 7 6 5 4 3 2 1

Printed on acid-free paper

Table of Contents

INTRODUCTION—VII

JANUARY

The Family Proclamation—1

FEBRUARY

Charity: The Pure Love of Christ—5

MARCH

Mission of the Holy Ghost—13

APRIL

The Resurrection of the Savior—21

MAY

Growing Our Testimonies—29

JUNE

Missionary Work: Fishers of Men—37

JULY

Pioneers: Gathering to Zion—45

AUGUST & SEPTEMBER

President Hinckley's "Be's"—55

OCTOBER

The Creation, the Fall, and the Atonement—67

NOVEMBER

Give Thanks unto God—75

DECEMBER

Prophecies of the Savior's Birth—83

BIBLIOGRAPHY—87

ABOUT THE AUTHOR—88

Introduction

Your family can learn to love and enjoy scripture study time together with these creative study themes. Each monthly theme uses fun, seasonal ideas to promote daily scripture study and teach basic gospel principles. Day after day, families read a set of themed scriptures and then work together to solve puzzles, answer questions, and build testimonies. Children will remember the lessons learned from scripture study as they have the opportunity to read the scriptures out loud and put together the monthly theme pieces.

By using these themes, you can help younger children be involved and look forward to studying the scriptures as a family. Start by copying (or printing pages from the accompanying CD) and cutting out the theme pieces. Use markers, colored pencils, crayons, scissors, glue, tape, and other simple supplies to prepare the monthly themes. Display the themes on a bulletin board, poster board, or kitchen cupboard. Once prepared, you are ready for an entire month of family scripture study sessions.

Offered with each theme are additional enrichment ideas that will help to enhance your family scripture study sessions. There are also suggestions that will help parents adapt the study themes to the ages and skill levels of their children.

Helpful Hints and Suggestions

1. Preparation is the key to simplifying a regular scripture study process. By spending approximately one hour preparing, your family will be ready for an entire month of scripture study sessions. For convenience, keep the theme pieces and tape or stapler near where you will be holding your family study sessions.

2. Use a bulletin board or other flat surface in a convenient area of the home to present the monthly scripture themes. Kids love to put the pieces up, and they enjoy seeing the changes throughout the month. Using a display surface in the dining area may help to make the scriptures become a point of discussion for meal times.

3. For most of these study themes, the actual scripture verses are included with the theme pieces. This eliminates the time needed to look up the verses in the standard works. However, for older children who may need experience looking up scriptures and finding references, parents may prefer to read only the scripture references to family members.

4. Repetition is one of the keys to learning. After introducing the monthly topic, ask your children the same question(s) about the theme prior to each study session. Repeat the question(s) daily until they are able to give the correct answer readily. For example, for the month of February and its theme, "Charity: The Pure Love of Christ," you may ask your children, "What is the theme this month?" or "How do the scriptures define charity?" Another good question is, "Who remembers what we learned about yesterday?"

5. Take time to define new words in the scriptures. Often the scriptural verses read differently than our modern language. Help clarify what the scriptures say by giving familiar examples and common definitions of terms or phrases.

January

The Family Proclamation

Objective: To help family members better understand "The Family: A Proclamation to the World" and how its counsel comes from the Lord through both ancient and latter-day prophets.

Directions: Enlarge the photo frame; the inner grid rectangle should measure 8" × 10". To make the picture puzzle, copy an 8" × 10" family photo onto cardstock. Cut the family photo into thirty equally sized squares (1.6" × 1.6"). Put the puzzle together by laying the pieces on the numbered grid in the photo frame poster. Number the back of each puzzle piece to match the numbers on the frame grid. Copy (or print pages from the accompanying CD) and cut out the squares containing the family proclamation quotes and supporting scriptures. Match these squares to the numbers on the back of the photo pieces and glue to secure. Laminate pieces for durability if desired. Have family members randomly select one puzzle piece each day. Read the portion of the family proclamation on the puzzle piece, followed by the supporting scripture, and discuss its meaning and impact. Place the puzzle piece on the grid by matching the numbers.

Optional Idea: Find a picture of a generic family in a magazine or book to copy and use. Do not show the complete picture to the family beforehand so it takes longer to figure out what the picture depicts.

Enrichment: Try to memorize the family proclamation by reciting from the beginning each day as the new sections are added. (This would require putting the puzzle pieces together in numerical order, rather than randomly as suggested above.) By the end of the month, family members should have the entire proclamation memorized.

Note: Since there are thirty-one days in January, but only thirty puzzle pieces, take the first day of the month to introduce the family proclamation and the new study theme.

Scriptures:

D&C 49:15	D&C 132:63	Jacob 3:10
Abraham 2:11	D&C 42:22	2 Nephi 25:26
Moses 6:8–9	2 Nephi 2:25	Mosiah 4:14–15
Romans 8:16–17	Moses 1:39	1 Timothy 5:8
Genesis 1:27	Moroni 8:17	Alma 57:21
Abraham 3:24–25	D&C 68:28	Proverbs 1:8
Abraham 3:26	D&C 134:5	D&C 136:8
D&C 130:2	D&C 68:25	Luke 17:2
D&C 132:19	Jeremiah 31:1	Alma 42:26
Genesis 1:28	1 Corinthians 11:11	D&C 134:1

The First Presidency and Council of the Twelve Apostles

The Church of Jesus Christ of Latter-day Saints

1	2	3	4	5
6	7	8	9	10
11	12	13	14	15
16	17	18	19	20
21	22	23	24	25
26	27	28	29	30

1. We, the First Presidency and the Council of the Twelve Apostles of The Church of Jesus Christ of Latter-day Saints, solemnly proclaim that marriage between a man and a woman is ordained of God . . . D&C 49:15	2. . . . and that the family is central to the Creator's plan for the eternal destiny of His children. Abraham 2:11	3. All human beings—male and female—are created in the image of God. Moses 6:8–9	4. Each is a beloved spirit son or daughter of heavenly parents, and, as such, each has a divine nature and destiny. Romans 8:16–17
5. Gender is an essential characteristic of individual premortal, mortal, and eternal identity and purpose. Genesis 1:27	6. In the premortal realm, spirit sons and daughters knew and worshipped God as their Eternal Father and accepted His plan by which His children could obtain a physical body and gain earthly experience Abraham 3:24–25	7. . . . to progress toward perfection and ultimately realize his or her divine destiny as an heir of eternal life. Abraham 3:26	8. The divine plan of happiness enables family relationships to be perpetuated beyond the grave. D&C 130:2
9. Sacred ordinances and covenants available in holy temples make it possible for individuals to return to the presence of God and for families to be united eternally. D&C 132:19	10. The first commandment that God gave to Adam and Eve pertained to their potential for parenthood as husband and wife. Genesis 1:28	11. We declare that God's commandment for His children to multiply and replenish the earth remains in force. D&C 132:63	12. We further declare that God has commanded that the sacred powers of procreation are to be employed only between man and woman, lawfully wedded as husband and wife. D&C 42:22
13. We declare the means by which mortal life is created to be divinely appointed. 2 Nephi 2:25	14. We affirm the sanctity of life and of its importance in God's eternal plan. Moses 1:39	15. Husband and wife have a solemn responsibility to love and care for each other and for their children. "Children are an heritage of the Lord" (Psalm 127:3). Moroni 8:17	16. Parents have a sacred duty to rear their children in love and righteousness, to provide for their physical and spiritual needs, to teach them to love and serve one another . . . D&C 68:28
17. . . . to observe the commandments of God and to be law-abiding citizens wherever they live. D&C 134:5	18. Husbands and wives—mothers and fathers—will be held accountable before God for the discharge of these obligations. D&C 68:25	19. The family is ordained of God. Jeremiah 31:1	20. Marriage between man and woman is essential to His eternal plan. 1 Corinthians 11:11

21. Children are entitled to birth within the bonds of matrimony, and to be reared by a father and a mother who honor marital vows with complete fidelity. Jacob 3:10	22. Happiness in family life is most likely to be achieved when founded upon the teachings of the Lord Jesus Christ. 2 Nephi 25:26	23. Successful marriages and families are established on principles of faith, prayer, repentance, forgiveness, respect, love, compassion, work, and wholesome recreational activities. Mosiah 4:14–15	24. By divine design, fathers are to preside over their families in love and righteousness and are responsible to provide the necessities of life and protection for their families. 1 Timothy 5:8
25. Mothers are primarily responsible for the nurture of their children. Alma 57:21	26. In these sacred responsibilities, fathers and mothers are obligated to help one another as equal partners. Proverbs 1:8	27. Disability, death, or other circumstances may necessitate individual adaptation. Extended families should lend support when needed. D&C 136:8	28. We warn that individuals who violate covenants of chastity, who abuse spouse or offspring, or who fail to fulfill family responsibilities will one day be held accountable before God. Luke 17:2
29. Further, we warn that the disintegration of the family will bring upon individuals, communities, and nations the calamities foretold by ancient and modern prophets. Alma 42:26	30. We call upon responsible citizens and officers of government everywhere to promote those measures designed to maintain and strengthen the family as the fundamental unit of society. D&C 134:1		

February

Charity: The Pure Love of Christ

Objective: To teach family members that charity is the pure love of Christ, about the importance of loving one another, and to follow the example of the Savior by treating others with compassion.

Directions: Make a copy of the valentine and scripture pages (or print pages from the accompanying CD), cut them out, and attach the scriptures to the back sides of the valentines. Color in the valentines. Laminate for durability if desired. Make a valentine mailbox by copying the "Love Letterbox" sign and attaching it to a shoebox or gift bag. Place the valentines inside. Remove one valentine each day and read the scripture on charity. Discuss the importance of the verse.

Optional Idea: Buy ready-made valentines and glue the scripture references to them. You can also purchase a mailbox to use, if preferred. Put the valentines in a small envelope and include a candy with each one!

Enrichment: Make a list of loved ones during the month, adding one new person to the list each day. Have each family member think of reasons they appreciate this person. You may even want to mail or give one of the valentines from the Love Letterbox to the loved ones on your list.

Scriptures:

1 Samuel 18:1	1 Corinthians 13:4–7	D&C 95:1
1 John 3:23	Jacob 3:2	1 Timothy 1:5
1 John 4:7–8	1 Corinthians 13:8	1 Peter 4:8
Mark 12:30–31	Ether 12:28	D&C 107:30
Luke 6:27–28	1 Corinthians 13:13	D&C 121:45
1 John 4:10–11	Ether 12:34	2 Peter 1:5–8
1 John 4:18	Colossians 3:14	Alma 7:24
John 14:15	D&C 12:8	1 Corinthians 13:1–3
John 15:12–13	Galations 5:22	Moroni 7:46–47

Love Letterbox

I treasure you, Valentine!

You're quite a catch, Valentine!

You'd make the "purr"-fect Valentine!

You're "T"-riffic, Valentine!

You're "toad"-ally awesome, Valentine!

I "chews" you to be my Valentine!

You're right on time to be my Valentine!

Valentine, you warm my heart!

And it came to pass, when he had made an end of speaking unto Saul, that the soul of Jonathan was knit with the soul of David, and Jonathan loved him as his own soul.
(1 Samuel 18:1)

And this is his commandment, That we should believe on the name of his Son Jesus Christ, and love one another, as he gave us commandment.
(1 John 3:23)

And thou shalt love the Lord thy God with all thy heart, and with all thy soul, and with all thy mind, and with all thy strength: this is the first commandment. And the second is like, namely this, Thou shalt love thy neighbour as thyself. There is none other commandment greater than these.
(Mark 12:30–31)

Beloved, let us love one another: for love is of God; and every one that loveth is born of God, and knoweth God. He that loveth not knoweth not God; for God is love.
(1 John 4:7–8)

But I say unto you which hear, Love your enemies, do good to them which hate you, Bless them that curse you, and pray for them which despitefully use you.
(Luke 6:27–28)

Herein is love, not that we loved God, but that he loved us, and sent his Son to be the propitiation for our sins. Beloved, if God so loved us, we ought also to love one another.
(1 John 4:10–11)

If ye love me, keep my commandments.
(John 14:15)

There is no fear in love; but perfect love casteth out fear: because fear hath torment. He that feareth is not made perfect in love.
(1 John 4:18)

You bring color to my world with your friendship! Happy Valentine's Day!

If you "carrot" all, you'll be my Valentine!

I would never tire of you, Valentine!

Must I beg? Please be mine!

My wish for you is a happy Valentine's Day!

You're very sweet to me, Valentine!

There's no "sub"-stitute for you, Valentine!

You're very "deer" to me!

Though I speak with the tongues of men and of angels, and have not charity, I am become as sounding brass, or a tinkling cymbal. And though I have the gift of prophecy, and understand all mysteries, and all knowledge; and though I have all faith, so that I could remove mountains, and have not charity, I am nothing. And though I bestow all my goods to feed the poor, and though I give my body to be burned, and have not charity, it profiteth me nothing.
(1 Corinthians 13:1–3)

O all ye that are pure in heart, lift up your heads and receive the pleasing word of God, and feast upon his love; for ye may, if your minds are firm, forever.
(Jacob 3:2)

Charity suffereth long, and is kind; charity envieth not; charity vaunteth not itself, is not puffed up, Doth not behave itself unseemly, seeketh not her own, is not easily provoked, thinketh no evil; Rejoiceth not in iniquity, but rejoiceth in the truth; Beareth all things, believeth all things, hopeth all things, endureth all things.
(1 Corinthians 13:4–7)

And see that ye have faith, hope, and charity, and then ye will always abound in good works.
(Alma 7:24)

Charity never faileth: but whether there be prophecies, they shall fail; whether there be tongues, they shall cease; whether there be knowledge, it shall vanish away.
(1 Corinthians 13:8)

Behold, I will show unto the Gentiles their weakness, and I will show unto them that faith, hope and charity bringeth unto me—the fountain of all righteousness.
(Ether 12:28)

And now abideth faith, hope, charity, these three; but the greatest of these is charity.
(1 Corinthians 13:13)

And now I know that this love which thou hast had for the children of men is charity; wherefore, except men shall have charity they cannot inherit that place which thou hast prepared in the mansions of thy Father.
(Ether 12:34)

We "bee"-long together!

Honey, please be mine!

I don't mean to "bug" you,
but will you be mine?

Guess who-who wants to be your Valentine?

You make my heart flutter!

Some- "bunny" loves you!

I have "two lips" for you, Valentine!

You are my "sole" mate!

And above all these things put on charity, which is the
bond of perfectness.
(Colossians 3:14)

And no one can assist in this work except he shall be
humble and full of love, having faith, hope, and charity,
being temperate in all things, whatsoever shall be entrusted
to his care.
(D&C 12:8)

Now the end of the commandment is charity out of a pure
heart, and of a good conscience, and of faith unfeigned.
(1 Timothy 1:5)

Verily, thus saith the Lord unto you whom I love, and
whom I love I also chasten that their sins may be forgiven,
for with the chastisement I prepare a way for their deliverance in all things out of temptation, and I have loved you.
(D&C 95:1)

And above all things have fervent charity among yourselves:
for charity shall cover the multitude of sins.
(1 Peter 4:8)

The decisions of these quorums, or either of them, are to
be made in all righteousness, in holiness, and lowliness
of heart, meekness and long suffering, and in faith, and
virtue, and knowledge, temperance, patience, godliness,
brotherly kindness and charity.
(D&C 107:30)

And beside this, giving all diligence, add to your faith
virtue; and to virtue knowledge; And to knowledge temperance; and to temperance patience; and to patience godliness; And to godliness brotherly kindness; and to brotherly
kindness charity. For if these things be in you, and abound,
they make you that ye shall neither be barren nor unfruitful
in the knowledge of our Lord Jesus Christ.
(2 Peter 1:5–8)

Let thy bowels also be full of charity towards all men,
and to the household of faith, and let virtue garnish thy
thoughts unceasingly; then shall thy confidence wax strong
in the presence of God; and the doctrine of the priesthood
shall distil upon thy soul as the dews from heaven.
(D&C 121:45)

You're the apple of my eye, Valentine!

I couldn't "bear" Valentine's Day without you!

You hold the key to my heart!

I get the shivers around you, Valentine!

This is my commandment, That ye love one another, as I have loved you. Greater love hath no man than this, that a man lay down his life for his friends.
(John 15:12–13)

We love him because he first loved us.
(1 John 4:19)

But the fruit of the Spirit is love, joy, peace, longsuffering, gentleness, goodness, faith.
(Galatians 5:22)

Wherefore, my beloved brethren, if ye have not charity, ye are nothing, for charity never faileth. Wherefore, cleave unto charity, which is the greatest of all, for all things must fail—But charity is the pure love of Christ, and it endureth forever; and whoso is found possessed of it at the last day, it shall be well with him.
(Moroni 7:46–47)

March

Mission of the Holy Ghost

Objective: To help family members learn more about the Holy Ghost as a member of the Godhead and how to better recognize the feelings and promptings of the Holy Ghost.

Directions: Copy and enlarge the five kites onto colored cardstock and cut them out. Make three copies of the kite tail ribbons page and a copy of each of the scripture pages (or print pages from the accompanying CD). Color kite tail ribbons. Cut out ribbons and scriptures and glue or tape scriptures to back side of ribbons. Laminate kites and ribbons for durability if desired. Place the kites on a bulletin board or other display surface and attach a two-foot-long piece of yarn or string to the kites for the tails. Randomly select one scripture tail ribbon each day and have family members determine on which kite it should be placed (which part of the Holy Ghost's mission is being discussed by the scripture). Discuss the importance of the scripture and then have a family member attach the ribbon to the appropriate kite tail.

Optional Idea: For younger children, color code the kites and tail ribbons to enable easier matching. It may also be helpful to spend an entire week discussing only one of the kite topics, and then move on to another kite once completed.

Enrichment: Contemplate the following quote by Sheri Dew and encourage family members to apply her advice to their prayers:

> I remember a time in my twenties when I was desperate for guidance on a crucial decision. I had fasted and prayed and been to the temple many times, but the answer wasn't clear. In frustration, I told a friend that I just couldn't get an answer. His simple response took me by surprise: "Have you asked the Lord to teach you how He communicates with you?" I hadn't, but I began that day to pray that He would. (*The Lord Wants a Powerful People*, 35)

Scriptures:

Missions of the Holy Ghost				
Enlightens the Mind	**Guides and Protects**	**Comforts and Uplifts**	**Testifies of Christ**	**Cleans and Sanctifies**
Jacob 4:13	Ezekiel 36:27	D&C 6:23	2 Nephi 31:18	D&C 33:11
D&C 6:15	Alma 14:11	Romans 15:13	D&C 20:27	3 Nephi 9:20
1 Corinthians 2:9–10	John 16:13	Galatians 5:22–23	3 Nephi 28:11	2 Nephi 31:17
D&C 8:2–3	2 Nephi 32:5	Moses 6:61	1 Corinthians 12:3	3 Nephi 27:20
John 14:26	D&C 45:57	D&C 88:3	D&C 21:9	Alma 13:12
Moroni 10:5	1 Nephi 4:6	Romans 5:5	John 15:26	Romans 15:16

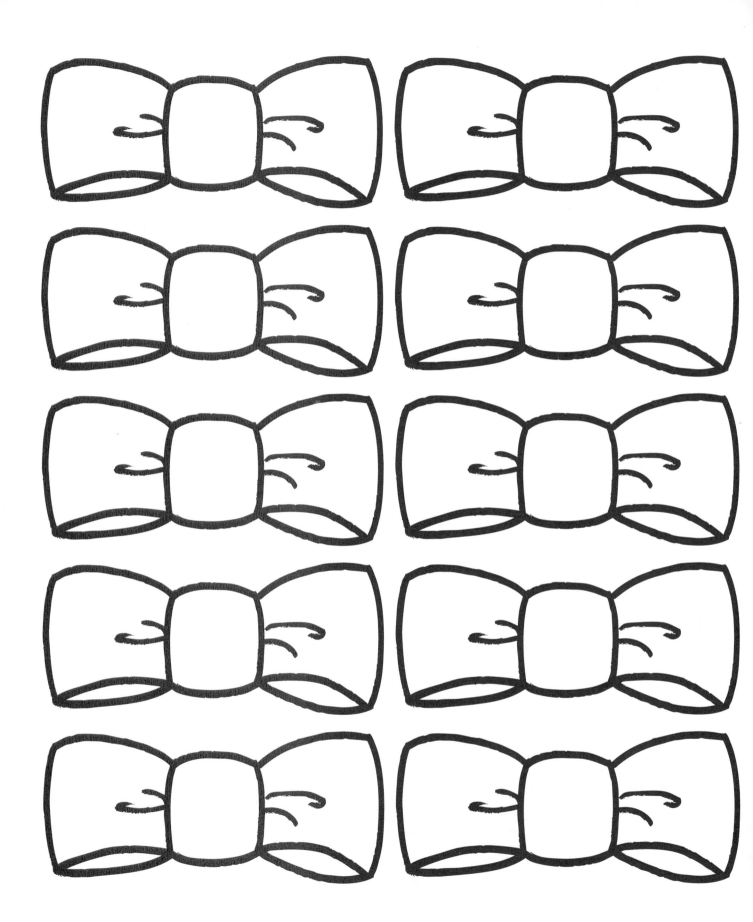

As well as those who should come after, who should believe in the gifts and callings of God by the Holy Ghost, which beareth record of the Father and of the Son.
(D&C 20:27)

Wherefore I give you to understand, that no man speaking by the Spirit of God calleth Jesus accursed: and that no man can say that Jesus is the Lord, but by the Holy Ghost.
(1 Corinthians 12:3)

But the Comforter, which is the Holy Ghost, whom the Father will send in my name, he shall teach you all things, and bring all things to your remembrance, whatsoever I have said unto you.
(John 14:26)

Yea, repent and be baptized, every one of you, for a remission of your sins; yea, be baptized even by water, and then cometh the baptism of fire and of the Holy Ghost.
(D&C 33:11)

Now the God of hope fill you with all joy and peace in believing, that ye may abound in hope, through the power of the Holy Ghost.
(Romans 15:13)

Wherefore, I now send upon you another Comforter, even upon you my friends, that it may abide in your hearts, even the Holy Spirit of promise; which other Comforter is the same that I promised unto my disciples.
(D&C 88:3)

And hope maketh not ashamed; because the love of God is shed abroad in our hearts by the Holy Ghost which is given unto us.
(Romans 5:5)

For they that are wise and have received the truth, and have taken the Holy Spirit for their guide, and have not been deceived—verily I say unto you, they shall not be hewn down and cast into the fire, but shall abide the day.
(D&C 45:57)

That I should be the minister of Jesus Christ to the Gentiles, ministering the gospel of God, that the offering up of the Gentiles might be acceptable, being sanctified by the Holy Ghost.
(Romans 15:16)

And by the power of the Holy Ghost ye may know the truth of all things.
(Moroni 10:5)

And ye shall offer for a sacrifice unto me a broken heart and a contrite spirit. And whoso cometh unto me with a broken heart and a contrite spirit, him will I baptize with fire and with the Holy Ghost.
(3 Nephi 9:20)

And the Holy Ghost beareth record of the Father and me; and the Father giveth the Holy Ghost unto the children of men, because of me.
(3 Nephi 28:11)

Now this is the commandment: Repent, all ye ends of the earth, and come unto me and be baptized in my name, that ye may be sanctified by the reception of the Holy Ghost, that ye may stand spotless before me at the last day.
(3 Nephi 27:20)

For, behold, I will bless all those who labor in my vineyard with a mighty blessing, and they shall believe on his words, which are given him through me by the Comforter, which manifesteth that Jesus was crucified . . . for the remission of sins unto the contrite heart.
(D&C 21:9)

Did I not speak peace to your mind concerning the matter? What greater witness can you have than from God?
(D&C 6:23)

Behold, thou knowest that thou hast inquired of me and I did enlighten thy mind; and now I tell thee these things that thou mayest know that thou hast been enlightened by the Spirit of truth.
(D&C 6:15)

For behold, again I say unto you that if ye will enter in by the way, and receive the Holy Ghost, it will show unto you all things what ye should do.
(2 Nephi 32:5)

And then are ye in this strait and narrow path which leads to eternal life; yea, ye have entered in by the gate; ye have done according to the commandments of the Father and the Son; and ye have received the Holy Ghost, which witnesses of the Father and the Son.
(2 Nephi 31:18)

For the gate by which ye should enter is repentance and baptism by water; and then cometh a remission of your sins by fire and by the Holy Ghost.
(2 Nephi 31:17)

But Alma said unto him: The Spirit constraineth me that I must not stretch forth mine hand; for behold the Lord receiveth them up unto himself, in glory.
(Alma 14:11)

Behold, my brethren, he that prophesieth, let him prophesy to the understanding of men; for the Spirit speaketh the truth and lieth not. Wherefore, it speaketh of things as they really are, and of things as they really will be.
(Jacob 4:13)

But as it is written, Eye hath not seen, nor ear heard, neither have entered into the heart of man, the things which God hath prepared for them that love him. But God hath revealed them unto us by his Spirit: for the Spirit searcheth all things, yea, the deep things of God.
(1 Corinthians 2:9–10)

And I will put my spirit within you, and cause you to walk in my statutes, and ye shall keep my judgments, and do them.
(Ezekiel 36:27)

But the fruit of the Spirit is love, joy, peace, longsuffering, gentleness, goodness, faith, Meekness, temperance: against such there is no law.
(Galatians 5:22–23)

Therefore it is given to abide in you; the record of heaven; the Comforter; the peaceable things of immortal glory.
(Moses 6:61)

But when the Comforter is come, whom I will send unto you from the Father, even the Spirit of truth, which proceedeth from the Father, he shall testify of me.
(John 15:26)

Howbeit when he, the Spirit of truth, is come, he will guide you into all truth: for he shall not speak of himself; but whatsoever he shall hear, that shall he speak: and he will shew you things to come.
(John 16:13)

And I was led by the Spirit, not knowing beforehand the things which I should do.
(1 Nephi 4:6)

Now they, after being sanctified by the Holy Ghost, having their garments made white, being pure and spotless before God, could not look upon sin save it were with abhorrence.
(Alma 13:12)

Yea, behold, I will tell you in your mind and in your heart, by the Holy Ghost, which shall come upon you and which shall dwell in your heart. Now, behold, this is the spirit of revelation.
(D&C 8:2–3)

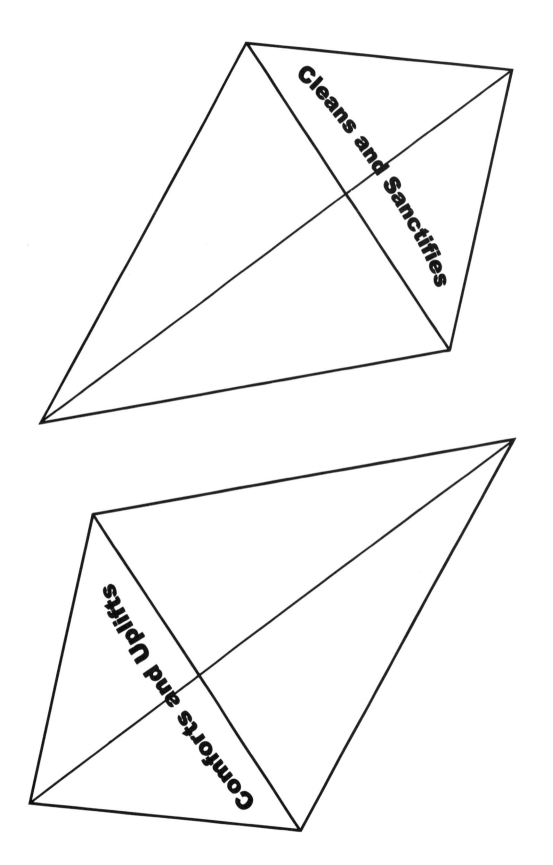

Cleans and Sanctifies

Comforts and Uplifts

18

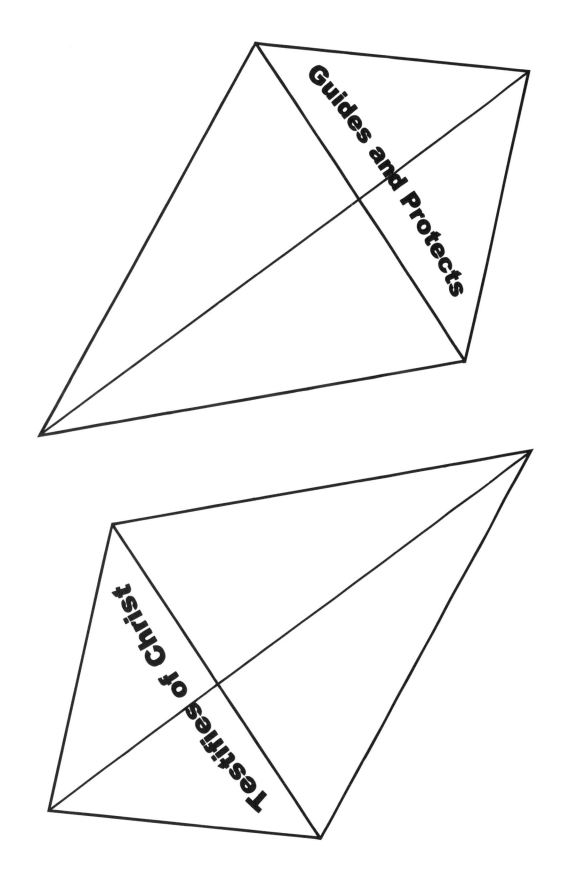

Guides and Protects

Testifies of Christ

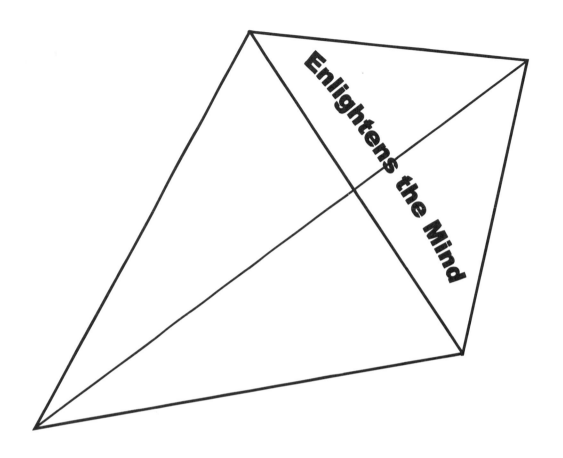

Enlightens the Mind

April

The Resurrection of the Savior

Objective: To help family members have a greater appreciation for the Savior's resurrection as an essential part of the plan of salvation and the reason for the Easter season.

Directions: Make five enlarged copies of the basket (or print pages from the accompanying CD) onto medium-heavy paper. Follow the folding directions to make the baskets. Copy the question signs onto cardstock and cut out. Attach a sign to each basket, then place the baskets on a display surface. Copy the scripture eggs onto patterned scrapbook paper, with words on the back side of the patterned paper, and then cut them out. Laminate the eggs for durability if desired. Hide the eggs for one of the baskets on the display surface or in the room. Show family members which Easter basket will be filled first and read the question on the basket. Have a family member find an egg each day and read the scripture. Discuss how the scripture helps to answer the question, then place the egg in the basket. After all six eggs are in the basket, move on to a new basket and repeat the process. Continue until all eggs are used.

Optional Idea: Use plastic Easter eggs, color coding the eggs by question; place the scripture verses inside, possibly with a small treat. Place all of the eggs in a basket and let a family member select an egg each day to read and discuss.

Enrichment: Practice singing the hymn "I Know That My Redeemer Lives" during each study session (*Hymns*, 136).

Note: On occasion Easter takes place in the month of March. When this happens, it may be appropriate to use the April theme during March to help emphasize the Easter season.

Scriptures:

Who made resurrection possible?	Who will be resurrected?	Why was Jesus Christ resurrected?	What happened when Jesus Christ was resurrected?	What will our bodies be like once resurrected?
Mosiah 16:7–8	2 Nephi 9:6	Romans 6:23	Matthew 28:16–19	1 Corinthians 15:40–42
Alma 40:2–3	2 Nephi 9:22	Philippians 3:20–21	Mark 16:9–11	2 Nephi 9:13
Mormon 7:5	D&C 76:39	Mosiah 15:8–9	Luke 24:1–6	Alma 11:42–43
D&C 88:17	Moses 7:62	Helaman 14:16–17	Luke 24:38–39	Alma 40:23
John 11:25–26	Alma 11:44	D&C 18:11–12	Luke 24:41–43	Alma 11:45
1 Corinthians 15:20–22	Alma 12:8	D&C 88:14–16	John 20:19–20	D&C 130:18

Basket Folding Directions

1. Cut out the basket, including tabs to sides of the basket.
2. Fold paper horizontally along the line at the bottom of the basket. The mirror image of the basket bowl below the bottom of the basket should now double up behind the basket.
3. Fold side basket tabs toward the back side of the basket.
4. Unfold all folds and lay the basket printed side down, flat on surface.
5. Fold side basket tabs toward the inside of the basket bowl, while at the same time refolding the horizontal fold along the bottom of the basket. Tabs should now be tucked in between the front and back basket bowl pieces.
6. Glue the tabs to the front and back of the basket bowl to keep them in place.

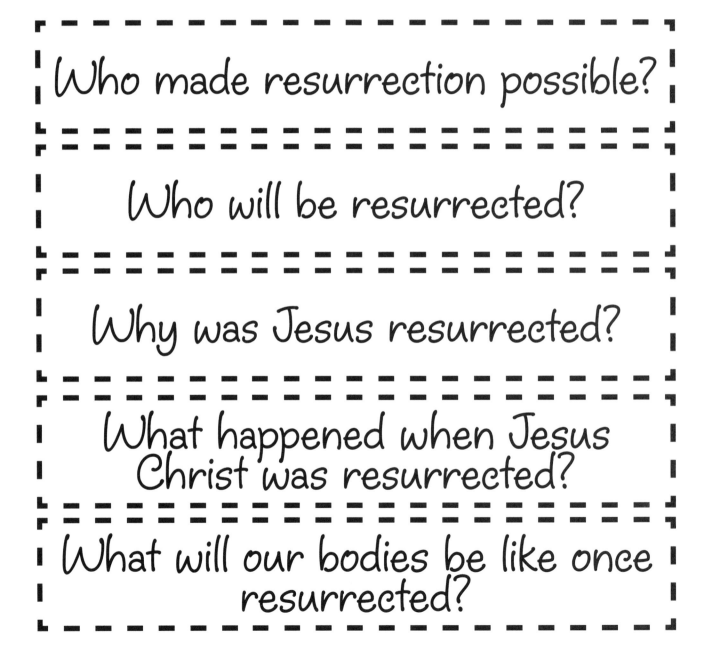

Who made resurrection possible?

Who will be resurrected?

Why was Jesus resurrected?

What happened when Jesus Christ was resurrected?

What will our bodies be like once resurrected?

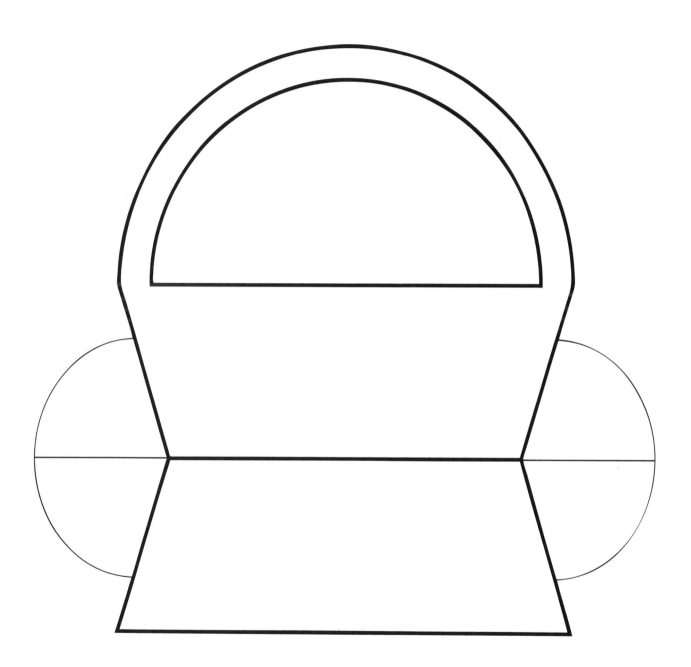

For as death hath passed upon all men, to fulfil the merciful plan of the great Creator, there must needs be a power of resurrection, and the resurrection must needs come unto man by reason of the fall; and the fall came by reason of transgression; and because man became fallen they were cut off from the presence of the Lord.
(2 Nephi 9:6)

And Zeezrom began to inquire of them diligently, that he might know more concerning the kingdom of God. And he said unto Alma: What does this mean which Amulek hath spoken concerning the resurrection of the dead, that all shall rise from the dead, both the just and the unjust, and are brought to stand before God to be judged according to their works?
(Alma 12:8)

Now, this restoration shall come to all, both old and young, both bond and free, both male and female, both the wicked and the righteous; and even there shall not so much as a hair of their heads be lost; but every thing shall be restored to its perfect frame, as it is now, or in the body, and shall be brought and be arraigned before the bar of Christ the Son, and God the Father, and the Holy Spirit, which is one Eternal God, to be judged according to their works, whether they be good or whether they be evil.
(Alma 11:44)

And righteousness will I send down out of heaven; and truth will I send forth out of the earth, to bear testimony of mine Only Begotten; his resurrection from the dead; yea, and also the resurrection of all men; and righteousness and truth will I cause to sweep the earth as with a flood, to gather out mine elect from the four quarters of the earth, unto a place which I shall prepare.
(Moses 7:62)

And he suffereth this that the resurrection might pass upon all men, that all might stand before him at the great and judgment day.
(2 Nephi 9:22)

For all the rest shall be brought forth by the resurrection of the dead, through the triumph and the glory of the Lamb, who was slain, who was in the bosom of the Father before the worlds were made.
(D&C 76:39)

Jesus said unto her, I am the resurrection, and the life: he that believeth in me, though he were dead, yet shall he live: And whosoever liveth and believeth in me shall never die. Believest thou this?
(John 11:25–26)

Know ye that ye must come to the knowledge of your fathers, and repent of all your sins and iniquities, and believe in Jesus Christ, that he is the Son of God, and that he was slain by the Jews, and by the power of the Father he hath risen again, whereby he hath gained the victory over the grave; and also in him is the sting of death swallowed up.
(Mormon 7:5)

And if Christ had not risen from the dead, or have broken the bands of death that the grave should have no victory, and that death should have no sting, there could have been no resurrection. But there is a resurrection, therefore the grave hath no victory, and the sting of death is swallowed up in Christ.
(Mosiah 16:7–8)

But now is Christ risen from the dead, and become the firstfruits of them that slept. For since by man came death, by man came also the resurrection of the dead. For as in Adam all die, even so in Christ shall all be made alive.
(1 Corinthians 15:20–22)

And the redemption of the soul is through him that quickeneth all things, in whose bosom it is decreed that the poor and the meek of the earth shall inherit it.
(D&C 88:17)

Behold, I say unto you, that there is no resurrection—or, I would say, in other words, that this mortal does not put on immortality, this corruption does not put on incorruption—until after the coming of Christ. Behold, he bringeth to pass the resurrection of the dead. But behold, my son, the resurrection is not yet.
(Alma 40:2–3)

For the wages of sin is death; but the gift of God is eternal life through Jesus Christ our Lord.
(Romans 6:23)

For our conversation is in heaven; from whence also we look for the Saviour, the Lord Jesus Christ: Who shall change our vile body, that it may be fashioned like unto his glorious body, according to the working whereby he is able even to subdue all things unto himself.
(Philippians 3:20–21)

And thus God breaketh the bands of death, having gained the victory over death; giving the Son power to make intercession for the children of men—Having ascended into heaven, having the bowels of mercy; being filled with compassion towards the children of men; standing betwixt them and justice; having broken the bands of death, taken upon himself their iniquity and their transgressions, having redeemed them, and satisfied the demands of justice.
(Mosiah 15:8–9)

Yea, behold, this death bringeth to pass the resurrection, and redeemeth all mankind from the first death—that spiritual death; for all mankind, by the fall of Adam being cut off from the presence of the Lord, are considered as dead, both as to things temporal and to things spiritual. But behold, the resurrection of Christ redeemeth mankind, yea, even all mankind, and bringeth them back into the presence of the Lord.
(Helaman 14:16–17)

For, behold, the Lord your Redeemer suffered death in the flesh; wherefore he suffered the pain of all men, that all men might repent and come unto him. And he hath risen again from the dead, that he might bring all men unto him, on conditions of repentance.
(D&C 18:11–12)

Now, verily I say unto you, that through the redemption which is made for you is brought to pass the resurrection from the dead. And the spirit and the body are the soul of man. And the resurrection from the dead is the redemption of the soul.
(D&C 88:14–16)

Then the eleven disciples went away into Galilee, into a mountain where Jesus had appointed them. And when they saw him, they worshipped him: but some doubted. And Jesus came and spake unto them, saying, All power is given unto me in heaven and in earth. Go ye therefore, and teach all nations, baptizing them in the name of the Father, and of the Son, and of the Holy Ghost.
(Matthew 28:16–19)

Now when Jesus was risen early the first day of the week, he appeared first to Mary Magdalene, out of whom he had cast seven devils. And she went and told them that had been with him, as they mourned and wept. And they, when they had heard that he was alive, and had been seen of her, believed not.
(Mark 16:9–11)

Now upon the first day of the week, very early in the morning, they came unto the sepulchre, bringing the spices which they had prepared. . . . And they found the stone rolled away from the sepulchre. And they entered in, and found not the body of the Lord Jesus. And it came to pass. . . . behold, two men stood by them in shining garments: And as they were afraid, and bowed down their faces to the earth, they said unto them, Why seek ye the living among the dead? He is not here, but is risen.
(Luke 24:1–6)

And while they yet believed not for joy, and wondered, he said unto them, Have ye here any meat? And they gave him a piece of a broiled fish, and of an honeycomb. And he took it, and did eat before them.
(Luke 24:41–43)

And he said unto them, Why are ye troubled? and why do thoughts arise in your hearts? Behold my hands and my feet, that it is I myself: handle me, and see; for a spirit hath not flesh and bones, as ye see me have.
(Luke 24:38–39)

Then the same day at evening, being the first day of the week, when the doors were shut where the disciples were assembled for fear of the Jews, came Jesus and stood in the midst, and saith unto them, Peace be unto you. And when he had so said, he shewed unto them his hands and his side. Then were the disciples glad, when they saw the Lord.
(John 20:19–20)

There are also celestial bodies, and bodies terrestrial: but the glory of the celestial is one, and the
glory of the terrestrial is another. There is one glory of
the sun, and another glory of the moon, and another glory
of the stars: for one star differeth from another star in glory.
So also is the resurrection of the dead. It is sown in corruption; it is raised in incorruption.
(1 Corinthians 15:40–42)

O how great the plan of our God! For on
the other hand, the paradise of God must deliver
up the spirits of the righteous, and the grave deliver up
the body of the righteous; and the spirit and the body is
restored to itself again, and all men become incorruptible,
and immortal, and they are living souls, having a perfect
knowledge like unto us in the flesh, save it be that our
knowledge shall be perfect.
(2 Nephi 9:13)

Now, there is a death which is called
a temporal death; and the death of Christ
shall loose the bands of this temporal death, that all
shall be raised from this temporal death. The spirit and
the body shall be reunited again in its perfect form; both
limb and joint shall be restored to its proper frame, even as
we now are at this time; and we shall be brought to stand
before God, knowing even as we know now, and have
a bright recollection of all our guilt.
(Alma 11:42–43)

Now, behold, I have spoken unto
you concerning the death of the mortal body,
and also concerning the resurrection of the mortal
body. I say unto you that this mortal body is raised to
an immortal body, that is from death, even from the first
death unto life, that they can die no more; their spirits unit-
ing with their bodies, never to be divided; thus the whole
becoming spiritual and immortal, that they can no
more see corruption.
(Alma 11:45)

The soul shall be restored to the body, and the
body to the soul; yea, and every limb and joint shall be
restored to its body; yea, even a hair of the head shall not
be lost; but all things shall be restored to their proper and
perfect frame.
(Alma 40:23)

Whatever principle of intelligence we attain unto in this
life, it will rise with us in the resurrection.
(D&C 130:18)

May

Growing Our Testimonies

Objective: To help teach family members what a testimony is, how to gain a testimony, and how or when they can share their testimony.

Directions: Copy the flower center and petal pages (or print pages from the accompanying CD) onto colored cardstock and cut out. Laminate for durability if desired. Enlarge flowerpot onto poster-size paper. Begin with the first testimony statement below and have a family member attach the flower center to one of the stems with tape. Then read one of the associated scriptures on the flower petals and discuss how the scripture would complete the testimony sentence on the flower center. Have a family member place the petal, scripture side down, next to the flower center. Continue reading one scripture each day for the same flower until all six petals are in place.

Optional Idea: Place all centers and petals on the flower stems. Pluck off the petals one at a time to read the scriptures and discuss.

Enrichment: Consider the following statement by Joseph B. Wirthlin and challenge family members to share their testimony in fast and testimony meeting the month following this scripture study.

> We should be patient in developing and strengthening our testimonies. Rather than expecting immediate or spectacular manifestations, though they will come when needed, we should pray for a testimony, study the scriptures, follow the counsel of our prophet and other Church leaders, and live the principles of the gospel. Our testimonies then will grow and mature naturally, perhaps imperceptibly at times, until they become driving forces in our lives. (Joseph B. Wirthlin, "Patience, a Key to Happiness," *Ensign*, May 1987, 30)

Scriptures:

1. A testimony is . . .	2. I can gain a testimony by . . .	3. I have a testimony of . . .	4. My testimony grows when I . . .	5. I can share my testimony . . .
Knowledge from God (Matthew 16:17)	Pondering (D&C 9:8–9)	Heavenly Father (Alma 30:44)	Pray (1 Nephi 2:16)	In a journal (1 Nephi 1:16)
Belief in truth (Jacob 4:13)	Listening to the Holy Ghost (1 Corinthians 12:3)	Jesus Christ (D&C 76:22–24)	Study the scriptures (2 Timothy 3:16)	With family members (1 Nephi 2:17)
A witness of God (Mosiah 18:9)	Obeying (John 7:16–17)	Joseph Smith (2 Nephi 3:24)	Attend church meetings (Matthew 18:20)	As a missionary (Alma 31:5)
A reward for enduring (Ether 12:6)	Asking God in prayer (D&C 8:1–2)	Book of Mormon (D&C 20:8–11)	Fast (Helaman 3:35)	At work (Alma 18:36)
The spirit of prophecy (Revelation 19:10)	Studying the scriptures (Moroni 10:4)	Gospel restoration (Revelation 14:6)	Choose the right (Leviticus 26:3, 12)	With friends (John 15:15)
A gift (D&C 46:13, 26)	Fasting (Alma 5:46)	Priesthood (Alma 4:20)	Share it (D&C 50:22)	At church (Revelation 22:16)

Growing a Testimony

(1) Knowledge from God

And Jesus answered and said unto him, Blessed art thou, Simon Bar-jona: for flesh and blood hath not revealed it unto thee, but my Father which is in heaven.
(Matthew 16:17)

(1) The spirit of prophecy

And I fell at his feet to worship him. And he said unto me, See thou do it not: I am thy fellowservant, and of thy brethren that have the testimony of Jesus: worship God: for the testimony of Jesus is the spirit of prophecy.
(Revelation 19:10)

(1) A gift

To some it is given by the Holy Ghost to know that Jesus Christ is the Son of God, and that he was crucified for the sins of the world. . . . And all these gifts come from God, for the benefit of the children of God.
(D&C 46:13, 26)

(1) Belief in truth

The Spirit speaketh the truth and lieth not. Wherefore, it speaketh of things as they really are, and of things as they really will be; wherefore, these things are manifested unto us plainly, for the salvation of our souls. But behold, we are not witnesses alone in these things; for God also spake them unto prophets of old.
(Jacob 4:13)

(1) A reward for enduring

And now, I, Moroni, would speak somewhat concerning these things; I would show unto the world that faith is things which are hoped for and not seen; wherefore, dispute not because ye see not, for ye receive no witness until after the trial of your faith.
(Ether 12:6)

(1) A witness of God

Yea, and are willing to mourn with those that mourn; yea, and comfort those that stand in need of comfort, and to stand as witnesses of God at all times and in all things, and in all places that ye may be in, even until death, that ye may be redeemed of God, and be numbered with those of the first resurrection, that ye may have eternal life.
(Mosiah 18:9)

(2) Pondering

But, behold, I say unto you, that you must study it out in your mind; then you must ask me if it be right, and if it is right I will cause that your bosom shall burn within you; therefore, you shall feel that it is right. But if it be not right you shall have no such feelings, but you shall have a stupor of thought that shall cause you to forget the thing which is wrong.
(D&C 9:8–9)

(2) Asking God in prayer

Surely shall you receive a knowledge of whatsoever things you shall ask in faith, with an honest heart, believing. . . . Yea, behold, I will tell you in your mind and in your heart, by the Holy Ghost, which shall come upon you and which shall dwell in your heart.
(D&C 8:1–2)

(2) Listening to the Holy Ghost

Wherefore I give you to understand, that no man speaking by the Spirit of God calleth Jesus accursed: and that no man can say that Jesus is the Lord, but by the Holy Ghost.
(1 Corinthians 12:3)

(2) Obeying

Jesus answered them, and said, My doctrine is not mine, but his that sent me. If any man will do his will, he shall know of the doctrine, whether it be of God, or whether I speak of myself.
(John 7:16–17)

(2) Studying the scriptures

And when ye shall receive these things, I would exhort you that ye would ask God, the Eternal Father, in the name of Christ, if these things are not true; and if ye shall ask with a sincere heart, with real intent, having faith in Christ, he will manifest the truth of it unto you, by the power of the Holy Ghost.
(Moroni 10:4)

(2) Fasting

I say unto you [these things] are made known unto me by the Holy Spirit of God. Behold, I have fasted and prayed many days that I might know these things of myself. And now I do know of myself that they are true; for the Lord God hath made them manifest unto me by his Holy Spirit; and this is the spirit of revelation which is in me.
(Alma 5:46)

(3) Heavenly Father

The scriptures are laid before thee, yea, and all things denote there is a God; yea, even the earth, and all things that are upon the face of it, yea, and its motion, yea, and also all the planets which move in their regular form do witness that there is a Supreme Creator.
(Alma 30:44)

(3) Jesus Christ

After the many testimonies which have been given of him, this is the testimony, last of all, which we give of him: That he lives! For we saw him, even on the right hand of God; and we heard the voice bearing record that he is the Only Begotten of the Father—That by him, and through him, and of him, the worlds are and were created, and the inhabitants thereof are begotten sons and daughters unto God.
(D&C 76:22–24)

(3) Joseph Smith

And there shall rise up one mighty among them, who shall do much good, both in word and in deed, being an instrument in the hands of God, with exceeding faith, to work mighty wonders, and do that thing which is great in the sight of God, unto the bringing to pass much restoration unto the house of Israel, and unto the seed of thy brethren.
(2 Nephi 3:24)

(3) Book of Mormon

And gave him power from on high, by the means which were before prepared, to translate the Book of Mormon; Which contains a record of a fallen people, and the fulness of the gospel of Jesus Christ. . . . Which was given by inspiration, and is confirmed to others by the ministering of angels, and is declared unto the world by them—Proving to the world that the holy scriptures are true, and that God does inspire men and call them to his holy work in this age and generation, as well as in generations of old.
(D&C 20:8–11)

(3) Gospel restoration

And I saw another angel fly in the midst of heaven, having the everlasting gospel to preach unto them that dwell on the earth, and to every nation, and kindred, and tongue, and people.
(Revelation 14:6)

(3) Priesthood

Alma delivered up the judgment-seat to Nephihah, and confined himself wholly to the high priesthood of the holy order of God, to the testimony of the word, according to the spirit of revelation and prophecy.
(Alma 4:20)

(4) Pray

And it came to pass that
I, Nephi, being exceedingly young,
nevertheless being large in stature, and
also having great desires to know of the
mysteries of God, wherefore, I did cry unto
the Lord; and behold he did visit me, and
did soften my heart that I did believe all
the words which had been spoken by my
father; wherefore, I did not rebel against
him like unto my brothers.
(1 Nephi 2:16)

(4) Fast

Nevertheless they did fast and pray oft,
and did wax stronger and stronger in their
humility, and firmer and firmer in the faith
of Christ, unto the filling their souls with
joy and consolation.
(Helaman 3:35)

(4) Share it

Wherefore, he that preacheth and he that
receiveth, understand one another, and
both are edified and rejoice together.
(D&C 50:22)

(4) Attend church meetings

For where two or three are gathered
together in my name, there am I in the
midst of them.
(Matthew 18:20)

(4) Choose the right

If ye walk in my statutes, and keep my
commandments, and do them; And I will
walk among you, and will be your God,
and ye shall be my people.
(Leviticus 26:3, 12)

(4) Study the scriptures

All scripture is given by inspiration of
God, and is profitable for doctrine, for
reproof, for correction, for instruction in
righteousness.
(2 Timothy 3:16)

(5) In a journal

And now I, Nephi, do not make a full account of the things which my father hath written, for he hath written many things which he saw in visions and in dreams; and he also hath written many things which he prophesied and spake unto his children.
(1 Nephi 1:16)

(5) With family members

And I spake unto Sam, making known unto him the things which the Lord had manifested unto me by his Holy Spirit. And it came to pass that he believed in my words.
(1 Nephi 2:17)

(5) At church

I Jesus have sent mine angel to testify unto you these things in the churches.
(Revelation 22:16)

(5) As a missionary

And now, as the preaching of the word had a great tendency to lead the people to do that which was just—yea, it had had more powerful effect upon the minds of the people than the sword, or anything else, which had happened unto them—therefore Alma thought it was expedient that they should try the virtue of the word of God.
(Alma 31:5)

(5) At work

Now when Ammon had said these words, he began at the creation of the world, and also the creation of Adam, and told him all the things concerning the fall of man, and rehearsed and laid before him the records and the holy scriptures of the people, which had been spoken by the prophets, even down to the time that their father, Lehi, left Jerusalem.
(Alma 18:36)

(5) With friends

Henceforth I call you not servants; for the servant knoweth not what his lord doeth: but I have called you friends; for all things that I have heard of my Father I have made known unto you.
(John 15:15)

A

testimony is . . .

I can gain a

testimony by . . .

I can share

my testimony . . .

My

testimony grows

when I . . .

I have a

testimony of . . .

June

Missionary Work: Fishers of Men

Objective: As one of the three-fold missions of the Church, missionary work is a major theme in the scriptures. Use this month's theme to help family members understand what missionaries do and how they are blessed for their work.

Directions: Make five copies of the fish page (or print pages from the accompanying CD), and then cut out and color the fish. Copy each of the scripture pages, cut out, and attach scriptures to back side of fish. Laminate for durability if desired. Attach a paper clip to each of the fish by punching a hole near the mouth. Make a fishing pole by tying a piece of yarn to a pencil; for a hook, attach a strong magnet. Place the fish into a bowl and have family members go fishing for a scripture each day. For additional discussion, sort the catch into various groups by topic (what missionaries do, what missionaries preach, missionary work in the spirit world, callings to be missionaries, and the gospel is to be taught to all the world).

Optional Idea: Create an underwater scene on a bulletin board and add a scripture fish each day after reading and discussing each scripture's meaning. For sorting, group the fish into schools by topic.

Enrichment: Invite the missionaries to dinner or family home evening and report as a family what you are learning about missionary work. Ask them to share their thoughts on serving the Lord as full-time missionaries.

Scriptures:

Isaiah 52:7	Revelation 14:6	D&C 15:6
Jeremiah 16:16	Mosiah 18:20	D&C 11:21
Matthew 4:18–19	Alma 8:32	D&C 52:9–10
Matthew 24:14	Alma 16:18	D&C 58:64
Matthew 28:19–20	Alma 17:9	D&C 88:81
Luke 4:18	Alma 18:36	D&C 123:12–13
Luke 22:31–32	Alma 21:16	D&C 133:8–9
John 21:17	Alma 31:5	D&C 138:30
1 Peter 3:18–19	D&C 4:1–2	D&C 138:57
1 Peter 4:6	D&C 4:3–4	Moses 6:23

How beautiful upon the mountains are the feet of him that bringeth good tidings, that publisheth peace; that bringeth good tidings of good, that publisheth salvation; that saith unto Zion, Thy God reigneth!
(Isaiah 52:7)

Behold, I will send for many fishers, saith the Lord, and they shall fish them; and after will I send for many hunters, and they shall hunt them from every mountain, and from every hill, and out of the holes of the rocks.
(Jeremiah 16:16)

And Jesus, walking by the sea of Galilee, saw two brethren, Simon called Peter, and Andrew his brother, casting a net into the sea: for they were fishers. And he saith unto them, Follow me, and I will make you fishers of men.
(Matthew 4:18–19)

And this gospel of the kingdom shall be preached in all the world for a witness unto all nations; and then shall the end come.
(Matthew 24:14)

Go ye therefore, and teach all nations, baptizing them in the name of the Father, and of the Son, and of the Holy Ghost: Teaching them to observe all things whatsoever I have commanded you: and, lo, I am with you alway, even unto the end of the world.
(Matthew 28:19–20)

And the Lord said, Simon, Simon, behold, Satan hath desired to have you, that he may sift you as wheat: But I have prayed for thee, that thy faith fail not: and when thou art converted, strengthen thy brethren.
(Luke 22:31–32)

The Spirit of the Lord is upon me, because he hath anointed me to preach the gospel to the poor; he hath sent me to heal the brokenhearted, to preach deliverance to the captives, and recovering of sight to the blind, to set at liberty them that are bruised.
(Luke 4:18)

He saith unto him the third time, Simon, son of Jonas, lovest thou me? Peter was grieved because he said unto him the third time, Lovest thou me? And he said unto him, Lord, thou knowest all things; thou knowest that I love thee. Jesus saith unto him, Feed my sheep.
(John 21:17)

For Christ also hath once suffered for sins, the just for the unjust, that he might bring us to God, being put to death in the flesh, but quickened by the Spirit: By which also he went and preached unto the spirits in prison.
(1 Peter 3:18–19)

For for this cause was the gospel preached also to them that are dead, that they might be judged according to men in the flesh, but live according to God in the spirit.
(1 Peter 4:6)

Yea, even he commanded them that they should preach nothing save it were repentance and faith on the Lord, who had redeemed his people.
(Mosiah 18:20)

And it came to pass that they went forth and began to preach and to prophesy unto the people, according to the spirit and power which the Lord had given them.
(Alma 8:32)

And I saw another angel fly in the midst of heaven, having the everlasting gospel to preach unto them that dwell on the earth, and to every nation, and kindred, and tongue, and people. (Revelation 14:6)

Those priests who did go forth among the people did preach against all lyings, and deceivings, and envyings, and strifes, and malice, and revilings, and stealing, robbing, plundering, murdering, committing adultery, and all manner of lasciviousness, crying that these things ought not so to be. (Alma 16:18)

And it came to pass that they journeyed many days in the wilderness, and they fasted much and prayed much that the Lord would grant unto them a portion of his Spirit to go with them, and abide with them, that they might be an instrument in the hands of God to bring, if it were possible, their brethren, the Lamanites, to the knowledge of the truth. (Alma 17:9)

When Ammon had said these words, he began at the creation of the world, and also the creation of Adam, and told him all the things concerning the fall of man, and rehearsed and laid before him the records and the holy scriptures of the people, which had been spoken by the prophets, even down to the time that their father, Lehi, left Jerusalem. (Alma 18:36)

And they went forth whithersoever they were led by the Spirit of the Lord, preaching the word of God in every synagogue of the Amalekites, or in every assembly of the Lamanites where they could be admitted. (Alma 21:16)

And now, as the preaching of the word had a great tendency to lead the people to do that which was just—yea, it had had more powerful effect upon the minds of the people than the sword, or anything else, which had happened unto them—therefore Alma thought it was expedient that they should try the virtue of the word of God. (Alma 31:5)

Now
behold, a mar-
velous work is about
to come forth among the
children of men. Therefore, O ye
that embark in the service of God,
see that ye serve him with all your
heart, might, mind and strength,
that ye may stand blameless
before God at the last day.
(D&C 4:1–2)

Therefore, if ye
have desires to serve God
ye are called to the work; For
behold the field is white already to
harvest; and lo, he that thrusteth in
his sickle with his might, the same
layeth up in store that he perisheth
not, but bringeth salvation to
his soul.
(D&C 4:3–4)

Seek not to
declare my word, but first
seek to obtain my word, and
then shall your tongue be loosed;
then, if you desire, you shall have
my Spirit and my word, yea, the
power of God unto the convincing
of men.
(D&C 11:21)

And now,
behold, I say unto you,
that the thing which will be
of the most worth unto you will
be to declare repentance unto this
people, that you may bring souls
unto me, that you may rest with
them in the kingdom of my
Father.
(D&C 15:6)

And let them
journey from thence
preaching the word by the way,
saying none other things than that
which the prophets and apostles have
written, and that which is taught them
by the Comforter through the prayer
of faith. Let them go two by two, and
thus let them preach by the way in
every congregation.
(D&C 52:9–10)

For, verily, the
sound must go forth
from this place into all the
world, and unto the uttermost
parts of the earth—the gospel must
be preached unto every creature,
with signs following them that
believe.
(D&C 58:64)

Behold, I sent you out to testify and warn the people, and it becometh every man who hath been warned to warn his neighbor. (D&C 88:81)

There are many yet on the earth among all sects, parties, and denominations, who are blinded by the subtle craftiness of men, whereby they lie in wait to deceive, and who are only kept from the truth because they know not where to find it—Therefore, that we should waste and wear out our lives in bringing to light all the hidden things of darkness. (D&C 123:12–13)

Send forth the elders of my church unto the nations which are afar off; unto the islands of the sea; send forth unto foreign lands; call upon all nations. . . . This shall be their cry, and the voice of the Lord unto all people: Go ye forth unto the land of Zion, that the borders of my people may be enlarged, and that her stakes may be strengthened, and that Zion may go forth unto the regions round about. (D&C 133:8–9)

But behold, from among the righteous, he organized his forces and appointed messengers, clothed with power and authority, and commissioned them to go forth and carry the light of the gospel to them that were in darkness, even to all the spirits of men; and thus was the gospel preached to the dead. (D&C 138:30)

I beheld that the faithful elders of this dispensation, when they depart from mortal life, continue their labors in the preaching of the gospel of repentance and redemption, through the sacrifice of the Only Begotten Son of God, among those who are in darkness and under the bondage of sin in the great world of the spirits of the dead. (D&C 138:57)

And they were preachers of righteousness, and spake and prophesied, and called upon all men, everywhere, to repent; and faith was taught unto the children of men. (Moses 6:23)

July

Pioneers: Gathering to Zion

Objective: To help children appreciate the difficulties pioneers faced when crossing the plains and understand the strong desire of pioneers to follow the commandments to build Zion.

Directions: Make eight copies of the wagon page (or print pages from the accompanying CD) and cut out. Copy each of the scripture pages, cut out, and attach to back side of wagons. Laminate for durability if desired. Have a family member choose a wagon card to read during scripture time. Read both the scripture and the pioneer story. Discuss why the scripture is important and how it contributes to the monthly topic. Post each wagon card on a display surface. Repeat this same process daily, lining up the wagon cards horizontally to form a growing wagon train.

Optional Idea: Substitute some of the stories with personal stories of ancestors who journeyed to America or were converted to the gospel in more recent times. Emphasize that pioneers do not have to be only those who lived in the early days of the Church; rather, many are pioneers as the first members in their family who decide to be baptized.

Enrichment: Post a map of the pioneer trail where family members can see it. Point out prominent landmarks, using pictures if possible, to help family members gain an appreciation for the distance and terrain.

Scriptures:

Joshua 1:9	Matthew 24:13	D&C 24:8
Psalm 73:28	2 Corinthians 1:6	D&C 58:2
Psalm 95:3–6	1 Timothy 4:12	D&C 58:4
Isaiah 2:2–3	James 5:11	D&C 59:1–2
Isaiah 5:26	1 Nephi 2:10	D&C 64:33–34
Isaiah 35:10	1 Nephi 13:37	D&C 64:41–42
Isaiah 40:11	2 Nephi 31:20	D&C 101:5
Isaiah 51:3	D&C 4:1–2	D&C 103:13
Jeremiah 40:11	D&C 14:7	D&C 121:8
Ezekiel 22:14	D&C 128:22–23	
Matthew 5:16	D&C 136:7	

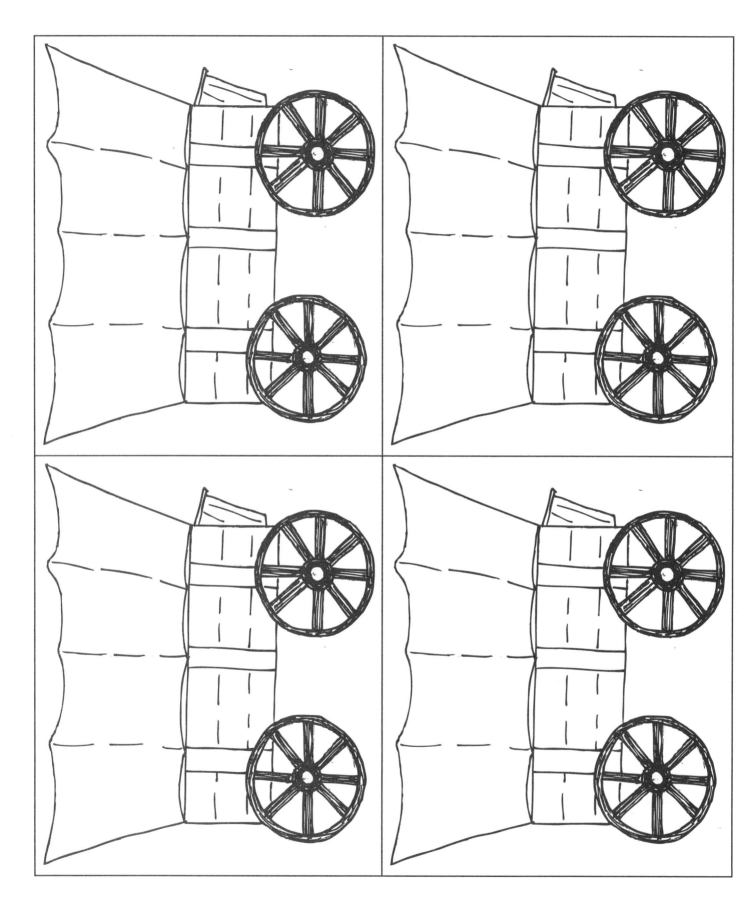

46

Behold, blessed, saith the Lord, are they who have come up unto this land with an eye single to my glory, according to my commandments. For those that live shall inherit the earth, and those that die shall rest from all their labors, and their works shall follow them; and they shall receive a crown in the mansions of my Father, which I have prepared for them. (D&C 59:1–2)

It was 1895, and the Farley family was moving from Snowflake, Arizona, to Provo, Utah. Before they left home, Father had filled all their barrels with water for both people and horses. He planned to refill them at springs along the way, but now the barrels were empty, and everyone was suffering. "We must rely on divine aid," Mother said firmly after another spring was found dry. "We have done all we can," Father prayed. "If it be Thy will that we should live, please send us water." Shortly after the prayer a cloud was spotted in the sky. They watched as the cloud grew larger and got closer. Soon it overshadowed them, and rain poured down. By the time the rain stopped, both animals and people had quenched their thirst. They all continued on their journey. "We have been part of a miracle," Father said reverently. (Adapted from Sheila Kindred, "Water in the Desert," *Friend*, July 2006, 4–6)

For, behold, I say unto you that Zion shall flourish, and the glory of the Lord shall be upon her; And she shall be an ensign unto the people, and there shall come unto her out of every nation under heaven. (D&C 64:41–42)

A lack of money was often a problem for those who wanted to join the Saints in the West. After 1849, many Latter-day Saints traveled to the Valley with help from the Perpetual Emigrating Fund. This fund loaned money to Church converts in Europe to enable them to emigrate to America and then on to Utah. Once they were established in their new homes and began to make a living, emigrants were to repay the loan, which enabled the Fund to continue its work of assistance. (*I Walked to Zion* [1994], 5)

Wherefore, be not weary in well-doing, for ye are laying the foundation of a great work. And out of small things proceedeth that which is great. Behold, the Lord requireth the heart and a willing mind; and the willing and obedient shall eat the good of the land of Zion in these last days. (D&C 64:33–34)

Agnes Caldwell was a pioneer in the Willie Handcart Company, which was caught in heavy storms and suffered terrible hunger and cold. Relief wagons came to deliver food and blankets, but there were not enough wagons to carry all the people. Little nine-year-old Agnes was too weary to walk any farther. A driver took notice of her determination to keep up with the wagon and asked if she would like a ride. "At this he reached over, taking my hand, clucking to his horses to make me run, with legs that . . . could run no farther. On we went, to what to me seemed miles. What went through my head at that time was that he was the meanest man that ever lived or that I had ever heard of. . . . Just at what seemed the breaking point, he stopped [and pulled me into the wagon]. Taking a blanket, he wrapped me up . . . warm and comfortable. Here I had time to change my mind, as I surely did, knowing full well by doing this he saved me from freezing when taken into the wagon." (Adapted from *I Walked to Zion* [1994], 58–59)

Now behold, a marvelous work is about to come forth among the children of men. Therefore, O ye that embark in the service of God, see that ye serve him with all your heart, might, mind and strength, that ye may stand blameless before God at the last day. (D&C 4:1–2)

One day while crossing the plains Hans Olsen Magleby noticed a large leather valise half buried in the dust along the trail. He picked it up and laid it in his handcart. After he had made camp that night, Hans opened the bag and found that it contained a lot of gold. Hans gave the bag to the head of the handcart company, Captain Rowley, and said nothing about it. A group of men from the gold fields of California came into camp a few days later. They told how they had lost a bag and wondered if anyone had seen it. Hans immediately spoke up and said he had found it. Captain Rowley gave the bag to the men. Because Hans had been honest, the men gave him $5 and a bag of salt. The gold miners said that the valise contained about $8000 in gold! But for Hans, being honest was more important than money. (Adapted from *The Life History of Hans Olsen Magleby* [1958], 13)

Wherefore, ye must press forward with a steadfastness in Christ, having a perfect brightness of hope, and a love of God and of all men. Wherefore, if ye shall press forward, feasting upon the word of Christ, and endure to the end, behold, thus saith the Father: Ye shall have eternal life. (2 Nephi 31:20)

Ellenor Roberts, a Welsh girl, was married to Elias Lewis under a shade tree at the Iowa outfitting camp. When loading their handcart they had to discard some of their precious belongings. Although the journey was a weary one they were cheerful and tried to be happy. As the journey continued, food became very scarce and many of their priceless possessions were traded for food. One of these was Ellenor's wedding ring, which was exchanged for flour. When they reached the Missouri River, Ellenor set her shoes on the bank to prepare for crossing. When she got to the other side she realized she had left the shoes behind. She walked the rest of the journey bare-footed. (Adapted from *Handcarts to Zion* [1992], 87)

And whether we be afflicted, it is for your consolation and salvation, which is effectual in the enduring of the same sufferings which we also suffer: or whether we be comforted, it is for your consolation and salvation. (2 Corinthians 1:6)

The real danger in crossing the plains was illness. . . . The second greatest danger to youngsters was accidents—the most common injuries being to children who fell beneath the wheels of moving wagons and handcarts. . . . Nervous parents tried to keep small children inside the wagons, but they soon became restless and curious and would hop in and out. Inevitably, a child would trip and hit the ground just as a wheel groaned over them. Gideon Murdock, age six, wrote, "I was not large enough to keep out of the way of the wagon at all times and consequently had my feet and leg run over two or three times when jumping out of the wagon to stop the team." (*I Walked to Zion* [1994], 8)

For the Lord shall comfort Zion: he will comfort all her waste places; and he will make her wilderness like Eden, and her desert like the garden of the Lord; joy and gladness shall be found therein, thanksgiving, and the voice of melody. (Isaiah 51:3)

For most, the Valley was a welcome sight, heralding not only the end of a tiresome journey but the beginning of a new life. Lucy Hannah White (Flake), who was eight years old at the time, wrote of her family's arrival in 1850: "That day happened to be mother's thirty-second birthday, and was a joyous occasion. I couldn't understand her tears. I said, 'Mother, your loved ones are here, you wanted to come, so why are you crying?' She squeezed my hand gently, and smiling through her tears answered, 'Lucy Hannah, when people are as happy as I am, they cannot keep from crying.'" (*I Walked to Zion* [1994], 9)

And the ransomed of the Lord shall return, and come to Zion with songs and everlasting joy upon their heads: they shall obtain joy and gladness, and sorrow and sighing shall flee away. (Isaiah 35:10)

William Clayton joined the Church in England in the early 1800s and was the leader of the first company of Saints journeying to Nauvoo. He was a trusted secretary of the Prophet Joseph Smith and a gifted violinist. He helped build the Nauvoo Concert Hall. In 1845, after the Prophet Joseph had been martyred and the Saints were preparing to move west, Brigham Young asked William Clayton to organize a brass band. The band's music lifted the hearts of the Saints at their evening camps. Sometimes the band performed concerts at settlements in Iowa in exchange for grain, supplies, or money for the Saints' journey. During this time he wrote the words to "All Is Well." The words of "All Is Well," written to an English melody, encouraged the pioneers. Soon it became almost a theme song. It was decided in the camps that when anyone started singing it, everyone would join in. Today "All Is Well" is known as the hymn "Come, Come Ye Saints." (Adapted from Pat Graham and Ruth Gardner, "Sharing Time: William Clayton and 'Come, Come, Ye Saints,'" *Friend*, July 1983, 36)

Turn, O backsliding children, saith the Lord; for I am married unto you: and I will take you one of a city, and two of a family, and I will bring you to Zion. (Jeremiah 40:11)

John Stucki was nine years old when he crossed the plains with his family. One day a chunk of buffalo meat was given to their family and John's father put it in the back of the cart, saying they would save the meat for Sunday dinner. John was so hungry and the meat smelled so good that he could not resist while pushing at the back of the handcart. John took his little pocket knife and whittled off a piece or two each day. When his father went to get the meat he came to John and asked him if he had been cutting off some of it. John was honest and said he had been so hungry he could not leave it alone. Instead of scolding him, John's father turned away and wiped tears from his eyes. (Adapted from *Handcarts to Zion* [1992], 189)

He shall feed his flock like a shepherd: he shall gather the lambs with his arm, and carry them in his bosom, and shall gently lead those that are with young. (Isaiah 40:11)

The best [wagons] were strong, yet lightweight. To help make them waterproof, pioneers covered the wooden bottom with tar and the white canvas top with oil. The top, which was stretched over five or six U-shaped bows, could be closed in the back using a drawstring if the weather was bad. Hooks on the inside and outside of the wagon held milk cans, tools, and women's bonnets. Spare wagon parts were stored underneath the flooring. (*Don't Know Much About the Pioneers* [2003], 17)

And, if you keep my commandments and endure to the end you shall have eternal life, which gift is the greatest of all the gifts of God. (D&C 14:7)

It took the Saints nine to eleven weeks on average to cross the plains using handcarts. The journey was about 1,400 miles in total, starting at Iowa City on the Missouri River. At first they would travel an average of fifteen miles a day, but as they grew stronger they could go as far as twenty to twenty-five miles per day. Companies were advised to leave Iowa City no later than the last week in June to ensure safe travel to Salt Lake before winter weather started. Some of the principle landmarks along the way were Council Bluffs, Devil's Gate, Fort Bridger, and Independence Rock.

Let no man despise thy youth; but be thou an example of the believers, in word, in conversation, in charity, in spirit, in faith, in purity. (1 Timothy 4:12)

[Pioneer] children worked hard doing many of the same chores as children do today, such as washing dishes, cleaning their rooms, and sweeping the floors. They also did chores that we almost never do, such as helping to make soap and butter. To make soap, they mixed lard and lye in a large brass kettle over a fire. Then they poured the mixture out and cut it into bars. To make butter, they separated cream from milk, put the cream into a churn, and turned the churn's handle until the cream hardened into butter.

In spite of all the work, the children still found time to play. In one popular game, they threaded string through two holes in a button or a wood chip, twirled the string to wind it up tightly, then alternately pulled and released the string to make the button spin. (Kristen J. Gough, "Exploring: Growing Up at Cove Fort," *Friend*, June 1998, 40)

O that thou mightest be like unto this valley, firm and steadfast, and immovable in keeping the commandments of the Lord! (1 Nephi 2:10)

Joseph F. Smith and his mother, Mary Fielding Smith, once had their best yoke of cattle go missing. Although Joseph and his uncle both searched for the cattle, they were not to be found. After praying for help, Mary set off to look for them. While walking through a tall field of grass, a herdsman told her he had seen the cattle in the opposite direction to which she was headed, but she ignored him and continued on. Soon she came to a deep ravine, in which she found the cattle tied up in a thick cluster of willows. The oxen had been fastened there during the night by some herdsmen who had the intention of stealing them and driving them to market. (Adapted from *I Walked to Zion* [1994], 36)

Can thine heart endure, or can thine hands be strong, in the days that I shall deal with thee? I the Lord have spoken it, and will do it. (Ezekiel 22:14)

The favorite vehicle for traveling across the plains was the white-topped wagon. This animal-drawn form of transportation also served as a mobile home. Families could use the wagons as kitchen and living rooms and sleep in and under them. Despite being packed with crates and barrels, the wagons were made more comfortable with oil lamps, rugs, pillows and even a little furniture. Boxes and bags of grain could be made into beds, and chests could serve as tables or chairs. Some arrangement in the wagon bed was often made for elderly or ill persons to rest, read, or knit as the vehicle bumped along the trail. (*I Walked to Zion* [1994], 5–6)

But it is good for me to draw near to God: I have put my trust in the Lord God, that I may declare all thy works. (Psalm 73:28)

Alice Cherrington was ten years old when she made the journey to Salt Lake City with her family in 1860. She wrote of this experience, "My father was very sick with mountain fever, which added to the hardships. When we reached Green River, there being so many of the family sick, Captain Smith decided to leave us to improve and rest up awhile. The station master had a good sized room which he let the family have to stay in while we were there. There were acres and acres of wild currants growing there. My father gathered them, my mother stewed them, and he ate so many of them they cured him of the mountain fever. We had very little provisions, a small portion of flour and a ham bone, was all we had. The station master was very good to us. One day he was going to a place called Wood River. My father had a watch he brought from England, which he asked the station master to take and trade or sell for provisions. He took the watch and brought the provisions father sent for, also the watch back." The Cherringtons later joined a handcart company and completed their journey to Zion. (Adapted from *Our Darton Ancestors* [2000], 178)

Behold, we count them happy which endure. Ye have heard of the patience of Job, and have seen the end of the Lord; that the Lord is very pitiful, and of tender mercy. (James 5:11)

The pioneers used horses, mules, oxen, and even milk cows to pull their wagons. Oxen were the most popular, preferred not for their great speed but for their strength and durability. They were less expensive to buy than horses, and they didn't require the more expensive equipment that horses used. Instead of harnesses, simple wooden yokes around their necks would do. A person "drove" oxen by walking along the left side behind the lead oxen and using a whip or prod to urge and guide them along. They were trained to respond to shouts of "gee" (right turn) and "haw" (left turn). Under normal conditions, oxen could pull a heavily loaded wagon two miles an hour. (*I Walked to Zion* [1994], 6)

Be patient in afflictions, for thou shalt have many; but endure them, for, lo, I am with thee, even unto the end of thy days. (D&C 24:8)

Indians frequently worried the travelers. And indeed, there were some tragic encounters. However, Indians helped the overland travelers more than they hurt them. Sixteen-year-old George Cunningham and his family were invited to camp one night with a large group of Omaha Indians at Wood River, Nebraska. "We did so and they were very friendly," he later wrote. Eighteen-year-old Stephen Forsdick watched as a man in his company traded a pint of sugar to a Pawnee Indian for a buffalo robe. Both parties were happy with the exchange. Simpson Montgomery Molen, who was fifteen, found that the Indians usually visited their camp "demanding presents as tokens of peace and friendship" but otherwise did no harm. (*I Walked to Zion* [1994], 7)

For after much tribulation come the blessings. Wherefore the day cometh that ye shall be crowned with much glory; the hour is not yet, but is nigh at hand. (D&C 58:4)

In 1847 Latter-day Saint pioneers were traveling across what is now the United States to find their promised land in the West. The Saints did not know exactly where they were supposed to go. Brigham Young was President of the Quorum of the Twelve Apostles at the time. He was the only one who knew where the Lord wanted them to establish Zion. But he was very ill. Wilford Woodruff drove the wagon as President Young rested in the back. As soon as President Young saw the desert valley of the Great Salt Lake, he told Elder Woodruff to stop and said, "This is the right place; for the Lord has shown it to me in a vision." (Adapted from "From the Life of President Wilford Woodruff: This Is the Place," *Friend*, July 2006, 10–11)

Let your light so shine before men, that they may see your good works, and glorify your Father which is in heaven. (Matthew 5:16)

Brigham Young laid out what the daily routine of each pioneer camp should be: "At 5 o'clock in the morning the bugle is to be sounded as a signal for every man to arise and attend prayers before he leaves his wagon. Then the people will engage in cooking, eating, feeding teams, etc., until seven o'clock, at which time the train is to move at the sound of the bugle. . . . At half past eight each evening the bugles are to be sounded again, upon which signal all will hold prayers in their wagons, and be retired to rest by nine o'clock." (Adapted from *I Walked to Zion* [1994], 105)

And he will lift up an ensign to the nations from far, and will hiss unto them from the end of the earth: and, behold, they shall come with speed swiftly. (Isaiah 5:26)

As a young pioneer girl, Ella's most treasured possession was a pretty cloth doll, whose face and hands were made of china. One morning the family was awakened early before daybreak and urged to break camp as quickly as possible. Still half asleep, Ella was placed in the wagon and continued sleeping for the next several hours. By the time she was fully awake, they were already several miles into their journey. It was then that she realized her doll was missing, but it was too late to go back for it. Her father heard her crying and asked what was wrong. Ella explained she had put the doll on a bed of pine needles at the foot of the big rock where they had camped the night before. He told her to stop crying and said he would go back to look for it. That night Ella sat down to watch for any sign of her father's return. When he finally arrived he walked up the hill toward her, with his hands behind him. He knelt down in front of her, looked into her eyes, and brought her precious dolly out from behind his back! (Adapted from Vaughn J. Featherstone, "Following in Their Footsteps," *Ensign*, July 1997, 8)

And it shall come to pass in the last days, that the mountain of the Lord's house shall be established in the top of the mountains, and shall be exalted above the hills; and all nations shall flow unto it. And many people shall go and say, Come ye, and let us go up to the mountain of the Lord, to the house of the God of Jacob; and he will teach us of his ways, and we will walk in his paths. (Isaiah 2:2–3)

One of the rules the pioneers had to follow was to be kind to their animals. Joseph F. Smith was especially kind to his animals and felt sorry for the oxen having to pull such heavy loads day after day. Later in his life, he told his own children, "My team leaders' names were Thom and Joe—we raised them from calves and they were both white. Thom was trim built, active, young and more intelligent than many a man . . . Thom was my favorite and best and most willing and obedient servant and friend. He was choice!" (Adapted from *The Lord Needed a Prophet* [1996], 95)

But he that shall endure unto the end, the same shall be saved. (Matthew 24:13)

When the pioneers arrived in the Salt Lake Valley, they planted wheat and other grain. They needed the grain to make bread and cereal to eat. The wheat grew big and tall. Just before it was time to harvest the wheat, a big cloud filled the sky. It was not a rain cloud, but a cloud of thousands of hungry black crickets. The crickets landed on the wheat and began to eat it. The pioneers did everything they could to stop the crickets from eating their wheat. They built fires, beat the crickets with brooms and blankets, and even tried covering the crickets with water. But the crickets did not stop. The pioneers were afraid that they would not have food for the winter. They knelt down and asked Heavenly Father for help. Soon great flocks of seagulls came and began to eat the crickets. Before long, most of the crickets were gone. The pioneers thanked Heavenly Father for sending the seagulls and saving their crops. (*Primary 1: I am a Child of God* [1994], 39)

And blessed are they who shall seek to bring forth my Zion at that day, for they shall have the gift and the power of the Holy Ghost; and if they endure unto the end they shall be lifted up at the last day, and shall be saved in the everlasting kingdom of the Lamb; and whoso shall publish peace, yea, tidings of great joy, how beautiful upon the mountains shall they be. (1 Nephi 13:37)

By 1856, the expense of outfitting several thousand immigrants each year with covered wagons and livestock was becoming too great for the pioneers and for the Church. Leaders decided to furnish immigrants with small two-wheeled carts, . . . which could be pulled and pushed by hand to the Salt Lake Valley. Although the Latter-day Saints did not invent this method of crossing the plains . . . their development of this method became the most remarkable travel experiment in the settlement of the American frontier. (*I Walked to Zion* [1994], 41)

Let each company, with their captains and presidents, decide how many can go next spring; then choose out a sufficient number of able-bodied and expert men, to take teams, seeds, and farming utensils, to go as pioneers to prepare for putting in spring crops. (D&C 136:7)

Pioneers packed their wagons with hundreds of pounds of food—per person! For each traveler, guides recommended bringing at least 200 pounds of flour, 75 pounds of bacon, 30 pounds of hardtack (hard bread), 25 pounds of sugar, 10 pounds of rice, 10 pounds of salt, . . . and various amounts of dried beans and fruit, baking soda, and cornmeal. (*Don't Know Much about the Pioneers* [2003], 16)

For all those who will not endure chastening, but deny me, cannot be sanctified. (D&C 101:5)

James Jensen, age sixteen, was in one of the handcart companies that came across to Salt Lake. One dark night . . . [he] was out in search of water, when he ran into an extensive bed of [prickly-pear] cacti. His feet, covered only with canvas soled socks, were soon filled with the sharp spines. When he could bear the pain no longer, he sat down to pull out the thorns; but he jumped up quicker than he sat; for he had sat on a healthy bed of prickly pears. The impressions remained deep in his memory. (Adapted from *Handcarts to Zion* [1992], 162)

And then, if thou endure it well, God shall exalt thee on high; thou shalt triumph over all thy foes. (D&C 121:8)

Benjamin F. Johnson was appointed one of the captains on the pioneer trail. As a company captain, it was his job to oversee 100 families during the journey. He also helped each family prepare by constructing wagons, finding teams, and purchasing food and supplies. However, when the time came to leave he still did not have enough supplies necessary for his own family for the crossing. President Brigham Young advised him to go to some of the men in his company for help. By following the prophet's counsel, Benjamin Johnson was able to get a wagon, a team of four oxen, and feed supplies within a few days. He was now ready to leave to cross the plains. (Adapted from *Benjamin F. Johnson: Friend to the Prophets* [1997], 61–62)

Behold, this is the blessing which I have promised after your tribulations, and the tribulations of your brethren—your redemption, and the redemption of your brethren, even their restoration to the land of Zion, to be established, no more to be thrown down. (D&C 103:13)

Young pioneers viewed the journey across the Great Plains very differently from adults. Some immigrant children saw their journey to the Salt Lake Valley as a delightful and exciting vacation. Alongside their family and friends, they energetically sang the songs of Zion, caught butterflies by day and fireflies by night, and learned to love the beauty and glory of the American West. (*I Walked to Zion* [1994], 6)

Brethren, shall we not go on in so great a cause? Go forward and not backward. Courage, brethren; and on, on to the victory! Let your hearts rejoice, and be exceedingly glad. . . . Let the mountains shout for joy, and all ye valleys cry aloud; and all ye seas and dry lands tell the wonders of your Eternal King! And ye rivers, and brooks, and rills, flow down with gladness. Let the woods and all the trees of the field praise the Lord; and ye solid rocks weep for joy! And let the sun, moon, and the morning stars sing together, and let all the sons of God shout for joy! And let the eternal creations declare his name forever and ever! (D&C 128:22–23)

Twelve-year-old Albert Dickson was just one of thousands of children pioneers who crossed the continent in the late 1840s and early 1850s. There were four other children in the Dickson family at that time who crossed the plains with Albert. In his journal he wrote, "We crossed the Missouri on a large flatboat. Two wagons went on each trip, with three men to the oar and one at the rear to steer. They would land down the river about one mile from the starting point, then pull the boat back with oxen." Albert found adventure in each new phase of the trip. (Adapted from Fay McCracken, "Children Pioneers," *Friend*, July 1995, 36)

For verily I say unto you, blessed is he that keepeth my commandments, whether in life or in death; and he that is faithful in tribulation, the reward of the same is greater in the kingdom of heaven. (D&C 58:2)

At dinner time Mama served the last few potatoes to Rhoda and her sister. Rhoda's father was serving a mission in England, and there was little food or money left for the family. Rhoda was asked to bless the food, and she asked the Lord to bless their father and help provide food for her family. A few minutes later Rhoda's brother burst through the door. "Quick! The Judds have turned the canal water into their ditches!" Everyone grabbed buckets to collect water that would help their crops grow in the summer heat. While collecting the water, Rhoda and her brother and sister found fish in the ditches. They took some back to show Mama. "But there have never been fish in that canal," Mama said quietly. "Children, this is a miracle. Just as he sent manna to the hungry Israelites, the Lord has sent fish for us to eat. And just like the children of Israel, we must gather all we can while there are fish to catch. Go and see if there are any more, and I will begin cleaning these and packing them in salt." (Adapted from Cindy Law, "Miracle of the Fishes," *Friend*, July 2003, 4)

For the Lord is a great God, and a great King above all gods. In his hand are the deep places of the earth: the strength of the hills is his also. The sea is his, and he made it: and his hands formed the dry land. O come, let us worship and bow down: let us kneel before the Lord our maker. (Psalm 95:3–6)

On the ship *International,* which left England in 1853, a group of 425 LDS immigrants were traveling to Zion. The ship also carried a number of unbaptized friends and relatives and a crew of 26. The ship ran into bad storms, delaying the crossing and making it necessary to ration food. In 4 weeks only one-third of the distance had been covered. Thanks to the faith and prayers of the valiant Saints, a miracle occurred: favorable winds made it possible to make up time lost. The ship docked after a 54-day voyage across the ocean. Christopher Arthur presided over the company of Latter-day Saints aboard the *International.* In his official report to the British Mission president, President Arthur wrote: "I am glad to inform you, that we have baptized all on board except 3 persons. . . . We can number the captain, first and second mates, with 18 of the crew, most of whom intend going right through to the valley. . . . The number baptized in all is 48, since we left our native shores." (Adapted from Robert L. Backman, "Faith in Every Footstep," *Ensign*, January 1997, 7)

Have not I commanded thee? Be strong and of a good courage; be not afraid, neither be thou dismayed: for the Lord thy God is with thee whithersoever thou goest. (Joshua 1:9)

While berry-picking along the pioneer trail, Lucy saw a funnel cloud approaching rapidly. Only once before had she seen such a cloud. When it had touched down, the tornado had ripped through their small farm in Nauvoo, destroying everything in its path. With her heart pounding, Lucy took her younger brother, Hyrum, by one hand and her sister, Eliza, by the other and began to run for shelter. The tornado gained on them, and Lucy prayed hard as she tried to get everyone to safety. Then she heard voice say, "Lie down in the gulch." At first she could not believe this would provide the shelter needed to protect them from the tornado, but then the voice came a second time. "Lie down now!" Lucy couldn't dismiss the voice this time. She pushed Hyrum and Eliza down and covered them with her own body. *Please, Heavenly Father,* Lucy prayed silently, *protect us from the tornado.* The voice came once more. "Do not fear. I am here." A sweet calm settled over her. When the tornado had passed, they got to their feet again and started toward the camp once more. (Adapted from Jane McBride Choate, "Lucy's Prayer," *Friend*, July 2001, 40)

August & September

President Hinckley's "Be's"

Objective: To build a scriptural foundation for the counsel given by President Gordon B. Hinckley, and to help children understand the value and blessings that come from being obedient to prophetic counsel.

Directions: Make eight copies of the bees (or print pages from the accompanying CD), then color and cut out. Copy each of the scripture pages, cut out, and attach to back side of bees. Enlarge a copy of the hive onto poster-size yellow paper. Laminate the bees, sign, and hive for durability if desired. Place the hive and sign on a bulletin board or other display surface. Starting with one of the "be" topics, have a family member choose a bee to read during scripture time. Discuss how the scripture is important and supports President Hinckley's counsel. Have a family member place the bee on or near the beehive. Read one scripture daily until finished with the first topic chosen; then start on a new topic. Repeat until all the topics and scripture bees have been read.

Optional Idea: Instead of using the hive provided, create a three-dimensional hive by stacking Styrofoam wreath floral pieces of graded diameters. Stack and attach wreaths together using toothpicks to anchor the pieces together. Cut a Styrofoam ball in half and place one half on top of the hive. Paint the Styrofoam hive yellow. Tape a toothpick to each photocopied bee and let family members stick the bee into the hive each day.

Enrichment: Read and study President Hinckley's talk when he first introduced the six "Be's," titled "A Prophet's Counsel and Prayer for Youth" (*Ensign*, January 2001, 2). Refer to his book *Way to Be* to study the additional three "Be's."

Scriptures:

Be Grateful	Be Smart	Be Clean	Be True	Be Humble
Mosiah 2:19	2 Nephi 9:28–29	Alma 5:19	Alma 5:45–46	Mosiah 21:14
Alma 26:8	2 Nephi 28:30	D&C 88:86	Alma 27:27	Alma 13:28
D&C 59:7	Alma 37:6	D&C 110:5	D&C 51:9	D&C 104:82
D&C 78:19	D&C 72:4	Articles of Faith 1:4	JS—H 1:25	D&C 112:10
1 Chronicles 16:8	D&C 88:40	2 Samuel 22:21	Articles of Faith 1:13	James 4:10
Psalm 136:26	1 Corinthians 3:19	Job 17:9	Luke 8:15	2 Chronicles 7:14
	James 1:5	Isaiah 1:16	Romans 13:13	Alma 32:16

Be Prayerful	Be Involved	Be Positive	Be Still
Alma 34:17–19	Alma 53:20	2 Nephi 2:24–25	Helaman 10:2
Alma 34:27	Moroni 7:13	2 Nephi 31:20	D&C 138:11
D&C 88:119	D&C 64:29	Ether 12:4	Mark 4:39
D&C 59:9	Luke 2:48–49	D&C 128:22	Luke 2:19
Matthew 21:21–22	Joshua 24:15	Proverbs 10:28	1 Kings 19:11–12
James 5:16	Proverbs 22:29	Isaiah 49:13	Job 37:14
Daniel 9:3		John 16:33	Psalm 46:10

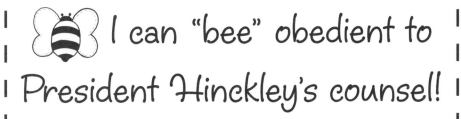 I can "bee" obedient to President Hinckley's counsel!

58

Be Prayerful

Yea, and when you do not cry unto the Lord, let your hearts be full, drawn out in prayer unto him continually for your welfare, and also for the welfare of those who are around you.
(Alma 34:27)

Be Prayerful

And that thou mayest more fully keep thyself unspotted from the world, thou shalt go to the house of prayer and offer up thy sacraments upon my holy day.
(D&C 59:9)

Be Prayerful

Therefore may God grant unto you, my brethren, that ye may begin to exercise your faith unto repentance, that ye begin to call upon his holy name, that he would have mercy upon you; Yea, cry unto him for mercy; for he is mighty to save. Yea, humble yourselves, and continue in prayer unto him.
(Alma 34:17–19)

Be Prayerful

Organize yourselves; prepare every needful thing; and establish a house, even a house of prayer, a house of fasting, a house of faith, a house of learning, a house of glory, a house of order, a house of God.
(D&C 88:119)

Be Prayerful

Confess your faults one to another, and pray one for another, that ye may be healed. The effectual fervent prayer of a righteous man availeth much.
(James 5:16)

Be Prayerful

Jesus answered and said unto them, Verily I say unto you, If ye have faith, and doubt not . . . . All things, whatsoever ye shall ask in prayer, believing, ye shall receive.
(Matthew 21:21–22)

Be Prayerful

And I set my face unto the Lord God, to seek by prayer and supplications, with fasting, and sackcloth, and ashes.
(Daniel 9:3)

Be Grateful

Give thanks unto the Lord, call upon his name, make known his deeds among the people.
(1 Chronicles 16:8)

Be Grateful

O give thanks unto the God of heaven: for his mercy
endureth for ever.
(Psalm 136:26)

Be Grateful

Thou shalt thank the Lord thy God in all things.
(D&C 59:7)

Be Grateful

And behold also, if I, whom ye call your king, who
has spent his days in your service, and yet has been
in the service of God, do merit any thanks from you,
O how you ought to thank your heavenly King!
(Mosiah 2:19)

Be Grateful

And he who receiveth all things with thankfulness shall
be made glorious; and the things of this earth shall be
added unto him, even an hundred fold, yea, more.
(D&C 78:19)

Be Grateful

Blessed be the name of our God; let us sing to his
praise, yea, let us give thanks to his holy name, for he
doth work righteousness forever.
(Alma 26:8)

Be Humble

Be thou humble; and the Lord thy God shall lead
thee by the hand, and give thee answer to thy prayers.
(D&C 112:10)

Be Humble

And inasmuch as ye are humble and faithful and call
upon my name, behold, I will give you the victory.
(D&C 104:82)

Be Humble

But that ye would humble yourselves before the
Lord, and call on his holy name, and watch and
pray continually, that ye may not be tempted above
that which ye can bear, and thus be led by the Holy
Spirit, becoming humble, meek, submissive, patient,
full of love and all long-suffering.
(Alma 13:28)

Be Humble

Humble yourselves in the sight of the Lord, and he shall lift you up.
(James 4:10)

Be Humble

Therefore, blessed are they who humble themselves without being compelled to be humble; or rather, in other words, blessed is he that believeth in the word of God, and is baptized without stubbornness of heart, yea, without being brought to know the word, or even compelled to know, before they will believe.
(Alma 32:16)

Be Humble

And they did humble themselves even in the depths of humility; and they did cry mightily to God; yea, even all the day long did they cry unto their God that he would deliver them out of their afflictions.
(Mosiah 21:14)

Be Humble

If my people, which are called by my name, shall humble themselves, and pray, and seek my face, and turn from their wicked ways; then will I hear from heaven, and will forgive their sin, and will heal their land.
(2 Chronicles 7:14)

Be Clean

I say unto you, can ye look up to God at that day with a pure heart and clean hands? I say unto you, can you look up, having the image of God engraven upon your countenances?
(Alma 5:19)

Be Clean

The righteous also shall hold on his way, and he that hath clean hands shall be stronger and stronger.
(Job 17:9)

Be Clean

The Lord rewarded me according to my righteousness: according to the cleanness of my hands hath he recompensed me.
(2 Samuel 22:21)

Be Clean

Wash you, make you clean; put away the evil of your doings from before mine eyes; cease to do evil.
(Isaiah 1:16)

Be Clean

Abide ye in the liberty wherewith ye are made free; entangle not yourselves in sin, but let your hands be clean, until the Lord comes.
(D&C 88:86)

Be Clean

Behold, your sins are forgiven you; you are clean before me; therefore, lift up your heads and rejoice.
(D&C 110:5)

Be Clean

We believe that the first principles and ordinances of the Gospel are: first, Faith in the Lord Jesus Christ; second, Repentance; third, Baptism by immersion for the remission of sins; fourth, Laying on of hands for the gift of the Holy Ghost.
(Articles of Faith 1:4)

Be True

And let every man deal honestly, and be alike among this people, and receive alike, that ye may be one, even as I have commanded you.
(D&C 51:9)

Be True

But that on the good ground are they, which in an honest and good heart, having heard the word, keep it, and bring forth fruit with patience.
(Luke 8:15)

Be True

Let us walk honestly, as in the day; not in rioting and drunkenness, not in chambering and wantonness, not in strife and envying.
(Romans 13:13)

Be True

Behold, I testify unto you that I do know that these things whereof I have spoken are true. And how do ye suppose that I know of their surety? Behold, I say unto you they are made known unto me by the Holy Spirit of God. Behold, I have fasted and prayed many days that I might know these things of myself.
(Alma 5:45–46)

Be True

And they were among the people of Nephi, and also numbered among the people who were of the church of God. And they were also distinguished for their zeal towards God, and also towards men; for they were perfectly honest and upright in all things; and they were firm in the faith of Christ, even unto the end.
(Alma 27:27)

Be True

We believe in being honest, true, chaste, benevolent, virtuous, and in doing good to all men; indeed, we may say that we follow the admonition of Paul—We believe all things, we hope all things, we have endured many things, and hope to be able to endure all things. If there is anything virtuous, lovely, or of good report or praiseworthy, we seek after these things.

(Articles of Faith 1:13)

Be True

I had actually seen a light, and in the midst of that light I saw two Personages, and they did in reality speak to me; and though I was hated and persecuted for saying that I had seen a vision, yet it was true; and while they were persecuting me . . . falsely for so saying, I was led to say in my heart: Why persecute me for telling the truth?

(JS—H 1:25)

Be Smart

For the wisdom of this world is foolishness with God. For it is written, He taketh the wise in their own craftiness.

(1 Corinthians 3:19)

Be Smart

If any of you lack wisdom, let him ask of God, that giveth to all men liberally, and upbraideth not; and it shall be given him.

(James 1:5)

Be Smart

O the vainness, and the frailties, and the foolishness of men! When they are learned they think they are wise, and they hearken not unto the counsel of God, for they set it aside, supposing they know of themselves, wherefore, their wisdom is foolishness and it profiteth them not. And they shall perish. But to be learned is good if they hearken unto the counsels of God.

(2 Nephi 9:28–29)

Be Smart

I will give unto the children of men line upon line, precept upon precept, here a little and there a little; and blessed are those who hearken unto my precepts, and lend an ear unto my counsel, for they shall learn wisdom; for unto him that receiveth I will give more; and from them that shall say, We have enough, from them shall be taken away even that which they have.

(2 Nephi 28:30)

Be Smart

Now ye may suppose that this is foolishness in me; but behold I say unto you, that by small and simple things are great things brought to pass; and small means in many instances doth confound the wise.

(Alma 37:6)

Be Smart

For he who is faithful and wise in time is accounted worthy to inherit the mansions prepared for him of my Father.

(D&C 72:4)

Be Smart

For intelligence cleaveth unto intelligence; wisdom receiveth wisdom; truth embraceth truth; virtue loveth virtue; light cleaveth unto light; mercy hath compassion on mercy and claimeth her own; justice continueth its course and claimeth its own; judgment goeth before the face of him who sitteth upon the throne and governeth and executeth all things.
(D&C 88:40)

Be Involved

Seest thou a man diligent in his business? he shall stand before kings; he shall not stand before mean men.
(Proverbs 22:29)

Be Involved

And they were all young men, and they were exceedingly valiant for courage, and also for strength and activity; but behold, this was not all—they were men who were true at all times in whatsoever thing they were entrusted.
(Alma 53:20)

Be Involved

Wherefore, as ye are agents, ye are on the Lord's errand; and whatever ye do according to the will of the Lord is the Lord's business.
(D&C 64:29)

Be Involved

And if it seem evil unto you to serve the Lord, choose you this day whom ye will serve; whether the gods which your fathers served that were on the other side of the flood, or the gods of the Amorites, in whose land ye dwell: but as for me and my house, we will serve the Lord.
(Joshua 24:15)

Be Involved

And when they saw him, they were amazed: and his mother said unto him, Son, why hast thou thus dealt with us? behold, thy father and I have sought thee sorrowing. And he said unto them, How is it that ye sought me? wist ye not that I must be about my Father's business?
(Luke 2:48–49)

Be Involved

But behold, that which is of God inviteth and enticeth to do good continually; wherefore, every thing which inviteth and enticeth to do good, and to love God, and to serve him, is inspired of God.
(Moroni 7:13)

Be Positive

But behold, all things have been done in the wisdom of him who knoweth all things. Adam fell that men might be; and men are, that they might have joy.
(2 Nephi 2:24–25)

Be Positive

Brethren, shall we not go on in so great a cause? Go forward and not backward. Courage, brethren; and on, on to the victory! Let your hearts rejoice, and be exceedingly glad. Let the earth break forth into singing. Let the dead speak forth anthems of eternal praise to the King Immanuel, who hath ordained, before the world was, that which would enable us to redeem them out of their prison; for the prisoners shall go free.
(D&C 128:22)

Be Positive

The hope of the righteous shall be gladness: but the expectation of the wicked shall perish.
(Proverbs 10:28)

Be Positive

These things I have spoken unto you, that in me ye might have peace. In the world ye shall have tribulation: but be of good cheer; I have overcome the world.
(John 16:33)

Be Positive

Sing, O heavens; and be joyful, O earth; and break forth into singing, O mountains: for the Lord hath comforted his people, and will have mercy upon his afflicted.
(Isaiah 49:13)

Be Positive

Wherefore, whoso believeth in God might with surety hope for a better world, yea, even a place at the right hand of God, which hope cometh of faith, maketh an anchor to the souls of men, which would make them sure and steadfast, always abounding in good works, being led to glorify God.
(Ether 12:4)

Be Positive

Wherefore, ye must press forward with a steadfastness in Christ, having a perfect brightness of hope, and a love of God and of all men. Wherefore, if ye shall press forward, feasting upon the word of Christ, and endure to the end, behold, thus saith the Father: Ye shall have eternal life.
(2 Nephi 31:20)

Be Still

And he said, Go forth, and stand upon the mount before the Lord. And, behold, the Lord passed by, and a great and strong wind rent the mountains, and brake in pieces the rocks before the Lord; but the Lord was not in the wind: and after the wind an earthquake; but the Lord was not in the earthquake: And after the earthquake a fire; but the Lord was not in the fire: and after the fire a still small voice.
(1 Kings 19:11–12)

Be Still

And as I pondered over these things which are written, the eyes of my understanding were opened, and the Spirit of the Lord rested upon me, and I saw the hosts of the dead, both small and great.
(D&C 138:11)

Be Still

And it came to pass that Nephi went his way towards
his own house, pondering upon the things which the
Lord had shown unto him.
(Helaman 10:2)

Be Still

And he arose, and rebuked the wind, and said unto
the sea, Peace, be still. And the wind ceased, and
there was a great calm. (Mark 4:39)

Be Still

Hearken unto this, O Job: stand still, and consider
the wondrous works of God.
(Job 37:14)

Be Still

But Mary kept all these things, and pondered them
in her heart.
(Luke 2:19)

Be Still

Be still, and know that I am God: I will be exalted
among the heathen, I will be exalted in the earth.
(Psalm 46:10)

October

The Creation, the Fall, and the Atonement

Objective: To teach family members about the three most important events in the plan of salvation, which enable us to come to earth, be tested, and to return to live with our Father once more.

Directions: Enlarge the tree onto poster-size paper. Make copies of the leaf pages (or print pages from the accompanying CD) on cardstock in fall colors. Cut out the leaves. Laminate the tree and leaves for durability if desired. Using a low tack masking tape, attach all of the leaves to the tree poster. Have a family member choose a leaf to read during scripture time. Discuss how the scripture is important and contributes to the monthly topic. Decide which topic the scripture is about (Creation, Fall, or Atonement) and place the leaf in the proper pile at the bottom of the poster. Continue reading one leaf each day and sorting the leaves into piles until all the leaves have "fallen" from the tree.

Optional Idea: When making the leaves, color code them by topic to help younger children. To challenge older children, make sure the colors are mixed up.

Enrichment: Consider the following quote from Russell M. Nelson and strive to teach family members how the Creation, Fall, and Atonement are all closely related and central to the plan of salvation.

A great council in heaven was once convened, in which it seems that all of us participated. There our Heavenly Father announced His plan. Scriptures refer to this plan of God by many names. . . . Prophets have used these terms interchangeably. Regardless of designation, the enabling essence of the plan is the atonement of Jesus Christ. As it is central to the plan, we should try to comprehend the meaning of the Atonement. Before we can comprehend it, though, we must understand the fall of Adam. And before we can fully appreciate the Fall, we must first comprehend the Creation. These three events—the Creation, the Fall, and the Atonement—are three preeminent pillars of God's plan, and they are doctrinally interrelated. (Russell M. Nelson, "Constancy amid Change," *Ensign*, November 1993, 33)

Scriptures:

Creation	Fall	Atonement
Genesis 1:26	Genesis 2:16–17	2 Nephi 2:26
Exodus 20:11	Genesis 3:4–5	Mosiah 3:11
Isaiah 42:5	2 Nephi 2:22	Mosiah 3:19
John 1:1–3	2 Nephi 2:23	Mosiah 4:7
Alma 22:12	2 Nephi 2:25	Alma 22:14
Mormon 9:12	Alma 42:7	3 Nephi 27:13–14
Ether 3:15	Alma 42:14	Mormon 9:13
Moses 3:7	Helaman 14:16	D&C 29:42
Abraham 3:24	D&C 29:40	D&C 76:40–42
Abraham 4:1	Moses 5:10	Moses 5:9
	Moses 6:48	

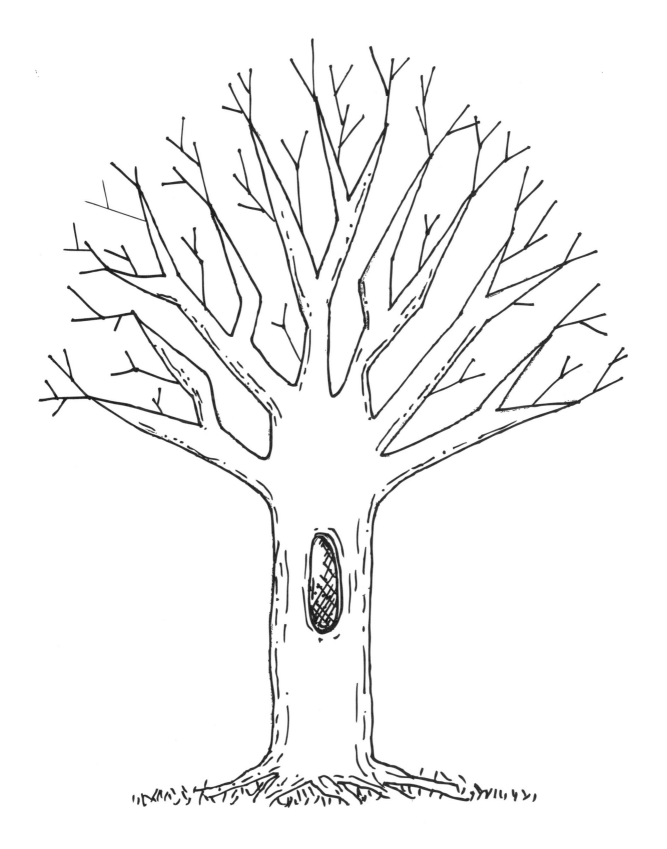

Creation Pile   Fall Pile   Atonement Pile

And God said, Let us make man in our image, after our likeness: and let them have dominion over the fish of the sea, and over the fowl of the air, and over the cattle, and over all the earth, and over every creeping thing that creepeth upon the earth. (Genesis 1:26)

And it came to pass that when Aaron saw that the king would believe his words, he began from the creation of Adam, reading the scriptures unto the king—how God created man after his own image, and that God gave him commandments, and that because of transgression, man had fallen. (Alma 22:12)

For in six days the Lord made heaven and earth, the sea, and all that in them is, and rested the seventh day: wherefore the Lord blessed the sabbath day, and hallowed it. (Exodus 20:11)

Behold, he created Adam, and by Adam came the fall of man. And because of the fall of man came Jesus Christ, even the Father and the Son; and because of Jesus Christ came the redemption of man. (Mormon 9:12)

Thus saith God the Lord, he that created the heavens, and stretched them out; he that spread forth the earth, and that which cometh out of it; he that giveth breath unto the people upon it, and spirit to them that walk therein. (Isaiah 42:5)

And never have I showed myself unto man whom I have created, for never has man believed in me as thou hast. Seest thou that ye are created after mine own image? Yea, even all men were created in the beginning after mine own image. (Ether 3:15)

In the beginning was the Word, and the Word was with God, and the Word was God. The same was in the beginning with God. All things were made by him; and without him was not any thing made that was made. (John 1:1–3)

And there stood one among them that was like unto God, and he said unto those who were with him: We will go down, for there is space there, and we will take of these materials, and we will make an earth whereon these may dwell. (Abraham 3:24)

And now, behold, if Adam had not transgressed he would not have fallen, but he would have remained in the garden of Eden. And all things which were created must have remained in the same state in which they were after they were created; and they must have remained forever, and had no end. (2 Nephi 2:22)

And then the Lord said: Let us go down. And they went down at the beginning, and they, that is the Gods, organized and formed the heavens and the earth. (Abraham 4:1)

And they would have had no children; wherefore they would have remained in a state of innocence, having no joy, for they knew no misery; doing no good, for they knew no sin. (2 Nephi 2:23)

And the Lord God commanded the man, saying, Of every tree of the garden thou mayest freely eat: But of the tree of the knowledge of good and evil, thou shalt not eat of it: for in the day that thou eatest thereof thou shalt surely die. (Genesis 2:16–17)

And I, the Lord God, formed man from the dust of the ground, and breathed into his nostrils the breath of life; and man became a living soul, the first flesh upon the earth, the first man also; nevertheless, all things were before created; but spiritually were they created and made according to my word. (Moses 3:7)

And the serpent said unto the woman, Ye shall not surely die: For God doth know that in the day ye eat thereof, then your eyes shall be opened, and ye shall be as gods, knowing good and evil. (Genesis 3:4–5)

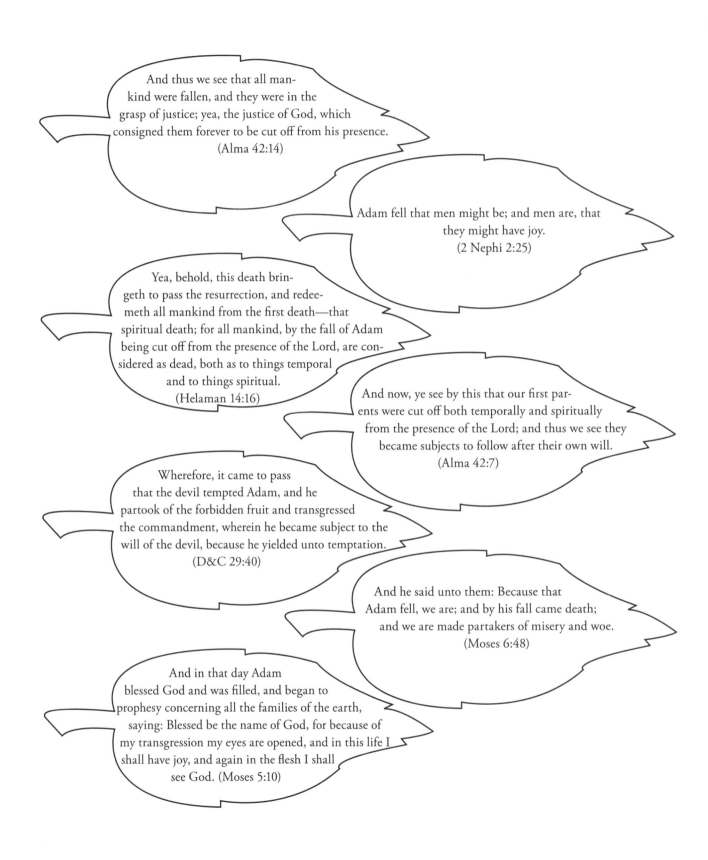

And thus we see that all mankind were fallen, and they were in the grasp of justice; yea, the justice of God, which consigned them forever to be cut off from his presence.
(Alma 42:14)

Adam fell that men might be; and men are, that they might have joy.
(2 Nephi 2:25)

Yea, behold, this death bringeth to pass the resurrection, and redeemeth all mankind from the first death—that spiritual death; for all mankind, by the fall of Adam being cut off from the presence of the Lord, are considered as dead, both as to things temporal and to things spiritual.
(Helaman 14:16)

And now, ye see by this that our first parents were cut off both temporally and spiritually from the presence of the Lord; and thus we see they became subjects to follow after their own will.
(Alma 42:7)

Wherefore, it came to pass that the devil tempted Adam, and he partook of the forbidden fruit and transgressed the commandment, wherein he became subject to the will of the devil, because he yielded unto temptation.
(D&C 29:40)

And he said unto them: Because that Adam fell, we are; and by his fall came death; and we are made partakers of misery and woe.
(Moses 6:48)

And in that day Adam blessed God and was filled, and began to prophesy concerning all the families of the earth, saying: Blessed be the name of God, for because of my transgression my eyes are opened, and in this life I shall have joy, and again in the flesh I shall see God. (Moses 5:10)

I say, that this is the man who receiveth salvation, through the atonement which was prepared from the foundation of the world for all mankind, which ever were since the fall of Adam, or who are, or who ever shall be, even unto the end of the world. (Mosiah 4:7)

And the Messiah cometh in the fulness of time, that he may redeem the children of men from the fall. And because that they are redeemed from the fall they have become free forever, knowing good from evil; to act for themselves and not to be acted upon, save it be by the punishment of the law at the great and last day, according to the commandments which God hath given. (2 Nephi 2:26)

And since man had fallen he could not merit anything of himself; but the sufferings and death of Christ atone for their sins, through faith and repentance, and so forth; and that he breaketh the bands of death, that the grave shall have no victory, and that the sting of death should be swallowed up in the hopes of glory. (Alma 22:14)

For behold, and also his blood atoneth for the sins of those who have fallen by the transgression of Adam, who have died not knowing the will of God concerning them, or who have ignorantly sinned. (Mosiah 3:11)

Behold I have given unto you my gospel, and this is the gospel which I have given unto you—that I came into the world to do the will of my Father, because my Father sent me. And my Father sent me that I might be lifted up upon the cross; and after that I had been lifted up upon the cross, that I might draw all men unto me. (3 Nephi 27:13–14)

For the natural man is an enemy to God, and has been from the fall of Adam, and will be, forever and ever, unless he yields to the enticings of the Holy Spirit, and putteth off the natural man and becometh a saint through the atonement of Christ the Lord. (Mosiah 3:19)

And because of the redemption of man, which came by Jesus Christ, they are brought back into the presence of the Lord; yea, this is wherein all men are redeemed, because the death of Christ bringeth to pass the resurrection, which bringeth to pass a redemption from an endless sleep. (Mormon 9:13)

But, behold, I say unto you
that I, the Lord God, gave unto Adam
and unto his seed, that they should not die as
to the temporal death, until I, the Lord God, should
send forth angels to declare unto them repentance and
redemption, through faith on the name of
mine Only Begotten Son.
(D&C 29:42)

And this is the gospel, the glad
tidings, which the voice out of the heavens
bore record unto us—That he came into the world,
even Jesus, to be crucified for the world, and to bear the
sins of the world, and to sanctify the world, and to cleanse it
from all unrighteousness; That through him all might be
saved whom the Father had put into his power
and made by him. (D&C 76:40–42)

And in that day the Holy
Ghost fell upon Adam, which beareth
record of the Father and the Son, saying: I am
the Only Begotten of the Father from the beginning,
henceforth and forever, that as thou hast fallen thou
mayest be redeemed, and all mankind, even
as many as will. (Moses 5:9)

November

Give Thanks unto God

Objective: To help family members recognize the importance of expressing gratitude to the Lord and to each other on a regular basis.

Directions: Enlarge the turkey onto poster-size paper and color, or piece a turkey together using cardstock paper. Make copies of the feather pages (or print pages from the accompanying CD) onto colored cardstock paper and cut out the feathers. Laminate for durability if desired. Starting with the larger feathers, have a family member choose a feather to read during scripture time. Discuss how the scripture is important and contributes to the monthly topic. After reading each feather, place it along the back of the turkey, scripture side down; overlap feathers slightly as needed. Use the shorter feathers after all of the larger ones have been read and place them in front of the larger feathers.

Optional Idea: Place all feathers on the turkey to start with and pluck one off each day to read. Or buy a bag of real colored feathers from a craft store and glue or staple them to the turkey each day after reading the scripture.

Enrichment: Have family members name one thing for which they are grateful after reading each scripture.

Scriptures:

1 Chronicles 16:8	Mosiah 18:23	Mosiah 2:19
Psalm 92:1–2	Alma 26:8	Mosiah 2:20
Psalm 136:1	D&C 46:32	Mosiah 26:39
Matthew 15:36	D&C 59:7	Alma 7:23
John 6:11	D&C 98:1	Alma 37:37
1 Corinthians 11:24	Ezra 3:11	Alma 45:1
1 Corinthians 15:57	Daniel 2:23	Mormon 9:31
Colossians 3:17	Daniel 6:10	Ether 6:9
1 Thessalonians 5:18	Luke 17:15–17	1 Nephi 5:9–10
2 Nephi 9:52	1 Thessalonians 2:13	
D&C 78:19	Jacob 4:3	

Give thanks unto the Lord, call upon his name, make known his deeds among the people.
(1 Chronicles 16:8)

It is a good thing to give thanks unto the Lord, and to sing praises unto thy name, O most High: To shew forth thy lovingkindness in the morning, and thy faithfulness every night.
(Psalm 92:1–2)

O give thanks unto the Lord; for he is good: for his mercy endureth for ever.
(Psalm 136:1)

And he took the seven loaves and the fishes, and gave thanks, and brake them, and gave to his disciples, and the disciples to the multitude.
(Matthew 15:36)

And he who receiveth all things with thankfulness shall be made glorious; and the things of this earth shall be added unto him, even an hundred fold, yea, more.
(D&C 78:19)

Condemn me not because of mine imperfection, neither my father, because of his imperfection, neither them who have written before him; but rather give thanks unto God that he hath made manifest unto you our imperfections, that ye may learn to be more wise than we have been.
(Mormon 9:31)

Behold, now it came to pass that the people of Nephi were exceedingly rejoiced, because the Lord had again delivered them out of the hands of their enemies; therefore they gave thanks unto the Lord their God; yea, and they did fast much and pray much, and they did worship God with exceedingly great joy.
(Alma 45:1)

And Jesus took the loaves; and when he had given thanks, he distributed to the disciples, and the disciples to them that were set down; and likewise of the fishes as much as they would.
(John 6:11)

And when he had given thanks, he brake it, and said, Take, eat: this is my body, which is broken for you: this do in remembrance of me.
(1 Corinthians 11:24)

But thanks be to God, which giveth us the victory through our Lord Jesus Christ.
(1 Corinthians 15:57)

And whatsoever ye do in word or deed, do all in the name of the Lord Jesus, giving thanks to God and the Father by him.
(Colossians 3:17)

Counsel with the Lord in all thy doings, and he will direct thee for good; yea, when thou liest down at night lie down unto the Lord, that he may watch over you in your sleep; and when thou risest in the morning let thy heart be full of thanks unto God; and if ye do these things, ye shall be lifted up at the last day.
(Alma 37:37)

And now I would that ye should be humble, and be submissive and gentle; easy to be entreated; full of patience and long-suffering; being temperate in all things; being diligent in keeping the commandments of God at all times; asking for whatsoever things ye stand in need, both spiritual and temporal; always returning thanks unto God for whatsoever things ye do receive.
(Alma 7:23)

And they did admonish their brethren; and they were also admonished, every one by the word of God, according to his sins, or to the sins which he had committed, being commanded of God to pray without ceasing, and to give thanks in all things.
(Mosiah 26:39)

In every thing give thanks: for this is the will of God in Christ Jesus concerning you.
(1 Thessalonians 5:18)

Blessed be the name of our God; let us sing to his praise, yea, let us give thanks to his holy name, for he doth work righteousness forever.
(Alma 26:8)

Behold, my beloved brethren, remember the words of your God; pray unto him continually by day, and give thanks unto his holy name by night. Let your hearts rejoice.
(2 Nephi 9:52)

And he commanded them that they should observe the sabbath day, and keep it holy, and also every day they should give thanks to the Lord their God.
(Mosiah 18:23)

And behold also, if I, whom ye call your king, who has spent his days in your service, and yet has been in the service of God, do merit any thanks from you, O how you ought to thank your heavenly King!
(Mosiah 2:19)

Now in this thing we do rejoice; and we labor diligently to engraven these words upon plates, hoping that our beloved brethren and our children will receive them with thankful hearts, and look upon them that they may learn with joy and not with sorrow, neither with contempt, concerning their first parents.
(Jacob 4:3)

And it came to pass that they did rejoice exceedingly, and did offer sacrifice and burnt offerings unto the Lord; and they gave thanks unto the God of Israel. And after they had given thanks unto the God of Israel, my father, Lehi, took the records which were engraven upon the plates of brass, and he did search them from the beginning.
(1 Nephi 5:9–10)

And ye must give thanks unto God in the Spirit
for whatsoever blessing ye are blessed with.
(D&C 46:32)

Thou shalt thank the Lord thy God in
all things.
(D&C 59:7)

For this cause also thank we God without ceasing, because, when ye received the word of God which ye heard
of us, ye received it not as the word of men, but as it is in truth, the word of God, which effectually worketh also
in you that believe.
(1 Thessalonians 2:13)

I thank thee, and praise thee, O thou God of my fathers, who hast given me wisdom and might, and hast
made known unto me now what we desired of thee: for thou hast now made known unto us the king's matter.
(Daniel 2:23)

Now when Daniel knew that the writing was signed, he went into his house; and his windows being open in
his chamber toward Jerusalem, he kneeled upon his knees three times a day, and prayed, and gave thanks before
his God, as he did aforetime.
(Daniel 6:10)

And they sang together by course in praising and giving thanks unto the Lord; because he is good, for his
mercy endureth for ever toward Israel. And all the people shouted with a great shout, when they praised the Lord,
because the foundation of the house of the Lord was laid.
(Ezra 3:11)

Verily I say unto you my friends, fear not, let your hearts be comforted; yea, rejoice evermore, and in everything give thanks.
(D&C 98:1)

And one of them, when he saw that he was healed, turned back, and with a loud voice glorified God, And fell down on his face at his feet, giving him thanks: and he was a Samaritan. And Jesus answering said, Were there not ten cleansed? but where are the nine?
(Luke 17:15–17)

And they did sing praises unto the Lord; yea, the brother of Jared did sing praises unto the Lord, and he did thank and praise the Lord all the day long; and when the night came, they did not cease to praise the Lord.
(Ether 6:9)

I say unto you, my brethren, that if you should render all the thanks and praise which your whole soul has power to possess, to that God who has created you, and has kept and preserved you, and has caused that ye should rejoice, and has granted that ye should live in peace one with another.
(Mosiah 2:20)

December

Prophecies of the Savior's Birth

Objective: To help focus the holiday season on the importance of the birth of the Savior and to teach family members of the many prophecies recorded in the scriptures regarding the birth of Jesus Christ.

Directions: Copy the gift tags (or print pages from the accompanying CD) and cut out. Laminate for durability if desired. Place the gift tags on a display surface (scripture side down) or in a festively wrapped gift box. Have a family member select a gift tag to read during scripture time. Discuss why the scripture is important and how it contributes to the monthly topic. Challenge family members to try and remember which prophet's prophecy was read the previous day.

Optional Idea: Punch holes in the center part of the tapered side of the gift tags. String a ribbon or piece of yarn through each hole. Place the gift tags on a small Christmas tree as decorations after each one is read.

Enrichment: Show family members a picture of each of the prophets when reading their prophecies regarding the Savior; use the Gospel Art Kit as a starting point. Additional artwork can be found in issues of the *Ensign* magazine or on LDS.org. A timeline may also be helpful to show family members when each prophet was alive.

Note: There are only thirty scriptures given for this month. Read the scriptural account of the Savior's birth in Luke 2 on Christmas Eve or Christmas Day in place of the scripture activity.

Scriptures:

Genesis 22:8	Zechariah 9:9	Micah 5:2
Genesis 49:10	Matthew 1:20–21	Alma 7:10
Deuteronomy 18:15	Luke 1:30–32	Alma 34:8
Numbers 24:17	1 Nephi 10:4	Alma 39:15
Psalm 89:26–27	1 Nephi 11:18–21	Helaman 8:13–15
Isaiah 7:14	2 Nephi 25:19	Helaman 8:19
Isaiah 9:6	Jacob 7:11–12	Helaman 14:2–3
Jeremiah 23:5	Enos 1:8	3 Nephi 1:13–14
Ezekiel 37:27	Mosiah 3:8	Ether 3:16
Hosea 13:4	Mosiah 15:1–2	Moses 6:57

For according to the words of the prophets, the Messiah cometh in six hundred years from the time that my father left Jerusalem; and according to the words of the prophets, and also the word of the angel of God, his name shall be Jesus Christ, the Son of God. (2 Nephi 25:19)

And he said unto me: Behold, the virgin whom thou seest is the mother of the Son of God, after the manner of the flesh. And it came to pass that I beheld that she was carried away in the Spirit . . . for the space of a time the angel spake unto me, saying: Look! And I looked and beheld the virgin again, bearing a child in her arms. And the angel said unto me: Behold the Lamb of God, yea, even the Son of the Eternal Father! (1 Nephi 11:18–21)

Yea, did [Moses] not bear record that the Son of God should come? And as he lifted up the brazen serpent in the wilderness, even so shall he be lifted up who should come. And as many as should look upon that serpent should live, even so as many as should look upon the Son of God with faith, having a contrite spirit, might live, even unto that life which is eternal. (Helaman 8:13–15)

And now I would that ye should know, that even since the days of Abraham there have been many prophets that have testified these things; yea, behold, the prophet Zenos did testify boldly; for the which he was slain. (Helaman 8:19)

Yea, even six hundred years from the time that my father left Jerusalem, a prophet would the Lord God raise up among the Jews—even a Messiah, or, in other words, a Savior of the world. (1 Nephi 10:4)

Behold, I say unto you that none of the prophets have written, nor prophesied, save they have spoken concerning this Christ. And this is not all—it has been made manifest unto me, for I have heard and seen; and it also has been made manifest unto me by the power of the Holy Ghost; wherefore, I know if there should be no atonement made all mankind must be lost. (Jacob 7:11–12)

And he said unto me: Because of thy faith in Christ, whom thou hast never before heard nor seen. And many years pass away before he shall manifest himself in the flesh; wherefore, go to, thy faith hath made thee whole. (Enos 1:8)

And he shall be called Jesus Christ, the Son of God, the Father of heaven and earth, the Creator of all things from the beginning; and his mother shall be called Mary. (Mosiah 3:8)

And now Abinadi said unto them: I would that ye should understand that God himself shall come down among the children of men, and shall redeem his people. And because he dwelleth in flesh he shall be called the Son of God, and having subjected the flesh to the will of the Father. (Mosiah 15:1–2)

And behold, he shall be born of Mary, at Jerusalem which is the land of our forefathers, she being a virgin, a precious and chosen vessel, who shall be overshadowed and conceive by the power of the Holy Ghost, and bring forth a son, yea, even the Son of God. (Alma 7:10)

My tabernacle also shall be with them: yea, I will be their God, and they shall be my people. (Ezekiel 37:27)

And now, behold, I will testify unto you of myself that these things are true. Behold, I say unto you, that I do know that Christ shall come among the children of men, to take upon him the transgressions of his people, and that he shall atone for the sins of the world; for the Lord God hath spoken it. (Alma 34:8)

The Lord thy God will raise up unto thee a Prophet from the midst of thee, of thy brethren, like unto me; unto him ye shall hearken. (Deuteronomy 18:15)

And now, my son, I would say somewhat unto you concerning the coming of Christ. Behold, I say unto you, that it is he that surely shall come to take away the sins of the world; yea, he cometh to declare glad tidings of salvation unto his people. (Alma 39:15)

I shall see him, but not now: I shall behold him, but not nigh: there shall come a Star out of Jacob, and a Sceptre shall rise out of Israel, and shall smite the corners of Moab, and destroy all the children of Sheth. (Numbers 24:17)

And behold, he said unto them: Behold, I give unto you a sign; for five years more cometh, and behold, then cometh the Son of God to redeem all those who shall believe on his name. And behold, this will I give unto you for a sign at the time of his coming; for behold, there shall be great lights in heaven, insomuch that in the night before he cometh there shall be no darkness, insomuch that it shall appear unto man as if it was day. (Helaman 14:2–3)

Yet I am the Lord thy God from the land of Egypt, and thou shalt know no god but me: for there is no saviour beside me. (Hosea 13:4)

Lift up your head and be of good cheer; for behold, the time is at hand, and on this night shall the sign be given, and on the morrow come I into the world, to show unto the world that I will fulfil all that which I have caused to be spoken by the mouth of my holy prophets. Behold, I come unto my own, to fulfil all things which I have made known unto the children of men from the foundation of the world, and to do the will, both of the Father and of the Son—of the Father because of me, and of the Son because of my flesh. And behold, the time is at hand, and this night shall the sign be given. (3 Nephi 1:13–14)

And Abraham said, My son, God will provide himself a lamb for a burnt offering: so they went both of them together. (Genesis 22:8)

Behold, this body, which ye now behold, is the body of my spirit; and man have I created after the body of my spirit; and even as I appear unto thee to be in the spirit will I appear unto my people in the flesh. (Ether 3:16)

The sceptre shall not depart from Judah, nor a lawgiver from between his feet, until Shiloh come; and unto him shall the gathering of the people be. (Genesis 49:10)

Rejoice greatly, O daughter of Zion; shout, O daughter of Jerusalem: behold, thy King cometh unto thee: he is just, and having salvation; lowly, and riding upon an ass, and upon a colt the foal of an ass. (Zechariah 9:9)

Behold, the days come, saith the Lord, that I will raise unto David a righteous Branch, and a King shall reign and prosper, and shall execute judgment and justice in the earth. (Jeremiah 23:5)

He shall cry unto me, Thou art my father, my God, and the rock of my salvation. Also I will make him my firstborn, higher than the kings of the earth. (Psalm 89:26–27)

For unto us a child is born, unto us a son is given: and the government shall be upon his shoulder: and his name shall be called Wonderful, Counsellor, The mighty God, The everlasting Father, The Prince of Peace. (Isaiah 9:6)

But while he thought on these things, behold, the angel of the Lord appeared unto him in a dream, saying, Joseph, thou son of David, fear not to take unto thee Mary thy wife: for that which is conceived in her is of the Holy Ghost. And she shall bring forth a son, and thou shalt call his name Jesus: for he shall save his people from their sins. (Matthew 1:20–21)

Therefore the Lord himself shall give you a sign; Behold, a virgin shall conceive, and bear a son, and shall call his name Immanuel. (Isaiah 7:14)

And the angel said unto her, Fear not, Mary: for thou hast found favour with God. And, behold, thou shalt conceive in thy womb, and bring forth a son, and shalt call his name Jesus. He shall be great, and shall be called the Son of the Highest: and the Lord God shall give unto him the throne of his father David. (Luke 1:30–32)

But thou, Beth-lehem Ephratah, though thou be little among the thousands of Judah, yet out of thee shall he come forth unto me that is to be ruler in Israel; whose goings forth have been from of old, from everlasting. (Micah 5:2)

Man of Holiness is his name, and the name of his Only Begotten is the Son of Man, even Jesus Christ, a righteous Judge, who shall come in the meridian of time. (Moses 6:57)

Bibliography

Backman, Robert L. "Faith in Every Footstep," *Ensign*, January 1997, 7.

Burr, Ruth and Wesley Burr, eds. *Our Darton Ancestors*. USA: The Darton Family Organization, 2000.

Choate, Jane McBride. "Lucy's Prayer," *Friend*, July 2001, 40.

Davis, Kenneth C. *Don't Know Much about the Pioneers*. New York: Harper Collins Publishers, 2003.

Dew, Sheri. *God Wants a Powerful People*. Salt Lake City: Deseret Book, 2007.

Featherstone, Vaughn J. "Following in Their Footsteps," *Ensign*, July 1997, 8.

"From the Life of President Wilford Woodruff: This is the Place," *Friend*, July 2006, 10–11.

Gough, Kristen J. "Growing Up at Cove Fort," *Friend*, June 1998, 40.

Graham, Pat and Ruth Gardner. "Sharing Time: William Clayton and 'Come, Come, Ye Saints,' " *Friend*, July 1983, 36.

Hafen, Le Roy R. and Ann W. Hafen. *Handcarts to Zion*. Spokane: Bison Book, 1992.

Hymns of The Church of Jesus Christ of Latter-day Saints. Salt Lake City: The Church of Jesus Christ of Latter-day Saints, 1985.

"I Am Grateful for Birds and Insects," *Primary 1: I Am a Child of God*. Salt Lake City: The Church of Jesus Christ of Latter-day Saints, 1994.

Kindred, Sheila. "Water in the Desert," *Friend*, July 2006, 4–6.

Law, Cindy. "Miracle of the Fishes," *Friend*, July 2003, 4.

LeBaron, E. Dale. *Benjamin F. Johnson: Friend to the Prophets*. Provo: Grandin Book Company, 1997.

The Life History of Hans Olsen Magleby. Salt Lake City: The Hans Olsen Memorial Foundation, 1958.

Madsen, Susan Arrington. *I Walked to Zion*. Salt Lake City: Deseret Book, 1994.

Madsen, Susan Arrington. *The Lord Needed a Prophet*. Salt Lake City: Deseret Book, 1996.

McCracken, Fay. "Exploring: Children Pioneers," *Friend*, July 1995, 36.

Nelson, Russell M. "Constancy amid Change," *Ensign*, November 1993, 33.

Wirthlin, Joseph B. "Patience, a Key to Happiness," *Ensign*, May 1987, 30.

About the Author

Rebecca Irvine lives in Mesa, Arizona. She is a graduate of Brigham Young University and served as a missionary for The Church of Jesus Christ of Latter-day Saints in the England London South Mission. Married for twelve years to her husband, Steve, she is the mother of three terrific children. Rebecca also works part-time as a market research analyst and volunteers as the research director for the Mesa Temple Easter Pageant.

Photograph by Carol Irvine.